Warrior • 18

Knight of Outre
AD 1187–1344

David Nicolle · Illustrated by Christa Hook

First published in Great Britain in 1996 by Osprey Publishing,
Midland House, West Way, Botley, Oxford OX2 0PH, UK
44-02 23rd St, Suite 219, Long Island City, NY 11101, USA
Email: info@ospreypublishing.com

Transferred to digital print on demand 2009

First published 1996
9th impression 2008

Printed and bound by Cadmus Communications, USA

A CIP catalogue record for this book is available from the British Library

ISBN: 978 1 85532 555 5

Editorial by Iain McGregor
Design by The Black Spot
Filmset in Great Britain by KDI, Newton le Willows
Typeset in Helvetica Neue and ITC New Baskerville

Dedication
For Suzanne and Georges-Eric, on a far distant shore though westward rather than easterly.

Artist's note
Readers may care to note that the original paintings from which the colour plates in this book were prepared are available for private
sale. All reproduction copyright whatsoever is retained by the Publishers. For further information visit:

www.gerryembleton.com

The Publishers regret that they can enter into no correspondence upon this matter.

KNIGHT of OUTREMER
AD 1187-1344

INTRODUCTION

Many books on the Crusades assume that the Crusader states in the Middle East were shadows of their former selves following Saladin's great victory at the battle of Hattin in 1187. Outremer, as medieval westerners called the remaining Latin or Catholic enclaves in the eastern Mediterranean, was no longer a threat to Islam and their military élites generally preferred to live in peace, focusing on trade as much as the defence of Christendom's holy places. Following the Crusade of 1239-41 the Kingdom of Jerusalem expanded again, but then fell back following the battle of La Forbie in 1244 – a disaster in that it was more final than Hattin. Thereafter fear of an alliance between the Crusaders and the Mongol invaders convinced the Mamluks to destroy the Latin states once and for all. But the fall of Acre in 1291 was not the end of the story. The Armenian Kingdom of Cilicia survived for almost a century while the Crusader Kingdom of Cyprus outlasted the Middle Ages. Another Outremer had meanwhile been created around the Aegean and eventually into the Black Sea following the Fourth Crusade of 1204. In fact Outremer only survived because Europeans dominated the seas while its gradual collapse usually resulted from insufficient manpower to hold fortified places. Nevertheless this fall still came as a terrible shock to Christendom.

CHRONOLOGY

1187 Muslims reconquer almost all the Kingdom of Jerusalem and other Crusader states.

1189 Kingdom of Jerusalem begins counter-attack.

1191 Richard I of England conquers Cyprus from Byzantines.

1204 Fourth Crusade captures Byzantine capital of Constantinople (Istanbul); establishment of the Latin Empire of Romania.

1229-33 Civil war in Latin Kingdom of Cyprus.

1244 Muslims (Khwarazmian freebooters) retake Jerusalem; defeat of Kingdom of Jerusalem at battle of La Forbie.

1256-58 Civil war in Kingdom of Jerusalem (War of St Sabas).

1261 Byzantines retake Constantinople (Istanbul) and much of southern Greece.

1268 Mamluks conquer Antioch, Jaffa and other parts of the Crusader states.

1271 Charles of Anjou, King of Naples and Sicily, recognized as King of Albania.

1277-78 Charles of Anjou buys Kingdom of Jerusalem and takes over Latin Principality of Achaea.

1282 Invasion of Sicily by Aragonese; start of Angevin-Neapolitan and Aragonese rivalry in eastern Mediterranean.

1286 Kingdom of Jerusalem under King of Cyprus.

1291 Muslims conquer Acre, end of Kingdom of Jerusalem.

1311 Catalan freebooters conquer Principality of Athens.

1334 Crusader League defeats Turks in Gulf of Edremit.

1344 Crusader League seizes Izmir from Turks.

Crusaders and residents

European knights had been taught to despise their Muslim foes as cowards who fought from a distance, supposedly because they had so little blood in their veins that they feared getting hurt. Such ludicrous propaganda decreased in the 13th century as the Church, and the more educated knights, came to see their enemies as heretics rather than pagans. Moral doubts prompted by contact with Islamic civilization were also expressed by a certain Ricoldus around 1294 when he wrote: 'We have been amazed that amongst the followers of so perfidious a law, deeds of so great perfection are to be found.' Meanwhile anti-Byzantine prejudice increased; Orthodox Greeks being portrayed as devious, cowardly and effete. Though the appeal of Crusading was fading fast, many knights remained a warlike breed. As the southern French troubadour Pierre de Bergerac sang around 1204:

I like to hear the rattling
*   Of the hauberk against the saddle-bow*
And to hear the tinkling and jingling of the harness bells,
*   Then I rush forward and see pourpoints and gambesons*
Thrown on top of armours.
*   The rustling of the pennons lifts my spirits.*
I know that hauberks and helmets and shields
*   Will have their day soon,*
And horses and lances and swords
*   And good vassals from this time on.*

Annales de Génes, late 12th/early 13th century. (Bib. Nat., Ms. Lat. 10134, Paris)
BELOW LEFT **Two-masted merchant ship of the type which carried Crusaders and supplies to the eastern Mediterranean.**
BELOW **War-galley or perhaps a horse-transport tarida with its mast and sail removed.**

The fact that many early Christian saints had been soldiers in the Roman Army appealed to the knightly class which adopted men like St George and St Maurice as their patron saints. The cult of St George was similarly encouraged by the Kingdom of Jerusalem because the saint's centre of pilgrimage was at Lydda, west of Jerusalem. As early as the 12th century the moralist Stephen of Muret tried to deal with the problems which faced a good knight who was in the service of a bad lord and wrote: 'It shows admirable knowledge and is very pleasing to God when a man who is involved in an evil enterprise restrains himself from evil. It can be done like this. If a knight is setting out on an expedition for the sake of his secular lord, to whom he cannot refuse obedience, if he wishes to be faithful to God let him first speak thus in his heart. Lord God, I will go on this expedition but I promise that I will be your knight there, wanting nothing in it except obedience to you, to eliminate evil and to seek after what is good in every occasion as much as I can.'

Though the Holy Land was seen as the supreme religious relic to be defended against Muslim reconquest, the catastrophic failure of successive Crusades undermined enthusiasm back in Europe. By the mid–13th century, leading Church thinkers like Humbert of Romans noted that those who preached the Crusade were often met with mockery while those who signed up often did so when drunk. Others went on Crusade to win a place in heaven despite their sins by obtaining an indulgence, in return for which a man agreed to serve for a specified period depending on his previous wickedness.

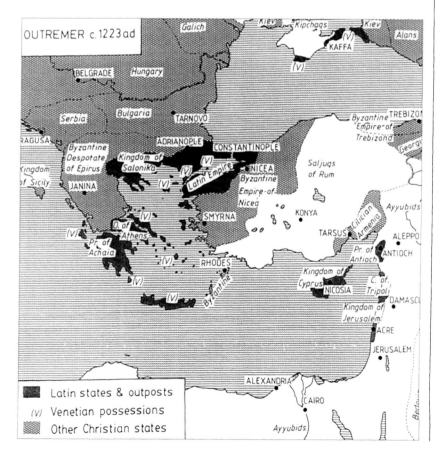

OUTREMER c.1223ad

Latin states & outposts
(v) Venetian possessions
Other Christian states

OUTREMER

By the 13th century the knightly class of Outremer had become a city-based coastal élite while the walled cities filled up as inland territory was lost, thus the population of the Latin states did not shrink as fast as its size. A widespread belief that the knights of Outremer had become degenerate was, however, unfounded. Many had slipped into poverty but in battle they still fought hard. On the other hand military leadership became confused as political authority fragmented.

The situation in the County of Tripoli was similar and in 1289 some of the city's élite considered putting themselves under Mamluk protection as a way of avoiding Genoese domination, though this was thwarted by the fanatical Templars. Antioch's situation was comparable though there had also been efforts to unify Antioch and Cilician Armenia, all of which failed. As a result Cilician Armenia now had several features in common with its Crusader neighbours. Meanwhile the Crusader Kingdom of Cyprus survived for the simple reason that it was an island. The Latin states established around the Aegean in the wake of the Fourth Crusade in 1204 also existed in a state of almost permanent war, their foes being Orthodox Christian Byzantines and Bulgarians. A partly Catholic, partly Orthodox Kingdom of Albania was set up by the French-Angevin rulers of southern Italy from 1272 to 1286, and again from 1304 until it was conquered by the Serbs in the 1340s.

Italian pirates infested the Aegean even before the Fourth Crusade and afterwards the smaller

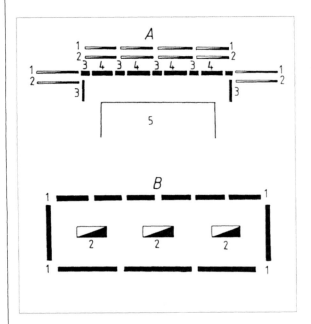

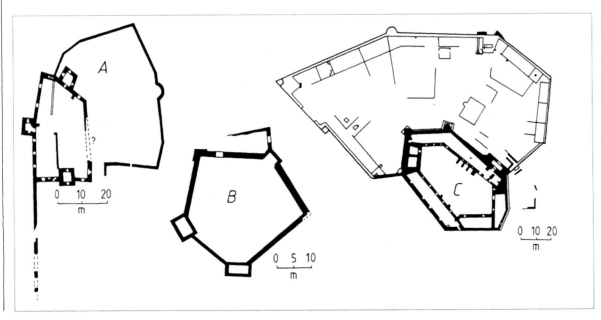

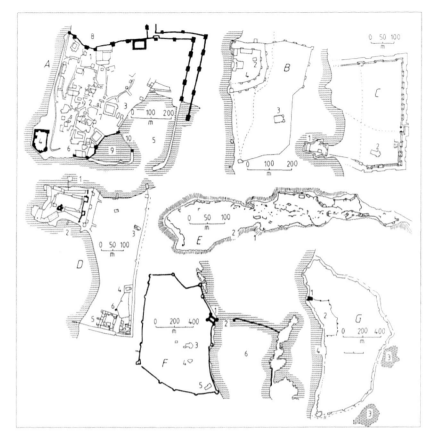

Aegean islands became meeting places for pirates of all origins except Muslims. Many of those involved were of knightly rank while troops who garrisoned Venetian and Genoese enclaves were almost entirely Italian in origin. By this time, however, the knightly élites of Italy and of the Italian enclaves in Outremer were very different from those of most of Western Europe. Here warfare was seen as a business where victory meant profit and defeat loss, with little room for abstract ideas of glory. Theoretically the defence of the Kingdom of Jerusalem was the joint responsibility of all Christian rulers but from the mid-13th century onwards the Italian merchant republics exercised a virtual protectorate over the Crusader states, drawing Outremer into the bitter rivalry of Venice and Genoa. By the second half of the 13th century the Latin states of Jerusalem, Tripoli and Antioch had, however, lost so much territory that they had to be supplied by sea with everything, even food. In return they sold Muslim slaves and luxury goods in transit from the Middle East, India or China.

THE KNIGHT IN OUTREMER

Western feudalism evolved in a situation of manpower surplus, but the opposite was the case in the Crusader states. In fact the conquest of western Syria and Palestine probably led to a general fall in population, just as happened when Spain, Portugal and Sicily fell to Christian

ABOVE **Partially defaced
Patriarchal Cross from the
keystone of an arch in the chapel
of Wu'aira castle in Jordan,
probably carved shortly before
Saladin's victory at the battle of
Hattin in 1187. (Author's photograph)**

The south-eastern corner of the fortified medieval city of Gibelet (now Jubail), the southernmost lordship in the County of Tripoli. (Author's photograph)

reconquest. As a result the knightly élite of Outremer was not only few in number but held fiefs with an inadequate number of peasants. Most of the élite were also of modest origins. Of almost 70 identifiable seigneurial families the great majority came from France, with a smaller number from the German Empire, the Norman kingdoms, Italy, Cilician Armenia and Latin Cyprus.

The acute shortage of manpower also led to a relaxation of the rules for knighthood to encourage pilgrims to settle. Such pilgrims came from as far afield as Iceland and Ethiopia. The Fourth Crusade led to another wave of settlement, though largely in the new Latin states around the Aegean. Knights who lived permanently in Outremer called themselves *chevaliers de la terre*, or 'knights of the land'. Those of mixed origin descended from a European father and a Middle Eastern mother, were called *poulains* or *polains* by westerners, possibly meaning colts or runts.

Another characteristic of Outremer, particularly in the 13th century, was the fact that most knights supported themselves with *fiefs en besants*, or 'money fiefs', rather than landed estates as in France; some drawing money from market tolls, industrial production or the sale of specific vegetables. A shortage of resident troops, combined with a relative abundance of cash, also led to a widespread use of mercenaries while the powerful Military Orders and urban communes also provided troops with knights. The nature of these 13th-century forces was changing, with the rising power of rich Italian merchants and knightly families being seen as a threat to the existing French-speaking knightly élite. For example, a Genoese knight of the Gatiluxius family and his four sons arrived in 1251, along with their weapons, horses and some followers aboard a merchant ship and a galley. Detailed information about others survives in a legal document dating from St Louis IX's Crusade a year earlier. The good ship *St Victor* had 453 Crusaders on board, eight of the ten leading passengers being knights together with a total of 90 retainers. Amongst them was Oliver de Termes, a southern French

Universal History of William of Tyre, Antioch, second half of the 13th century. (Bib. Apost., Ms. Pal. Lat. 1963, Rome) ABOVE LEFT **'Crusader army', showing a knight with an early form of great-helm. (f. 31v)** MIDDLE **'Crusader siege of Antioch.' (f. 40r)** RIGHT **'Bohemond entrusts Tancred with the government of Antioch and sails back to Italy.' In the upper register Bohemond gives Tancred his sword when handing over authority. (f.100r)**

knight who had found himself on the wrong side during the Albigensian Crusade. Once in Outremer, however, he carved out a new career and rose to command the élite 'French Regiment' of knights and cross-bowmen. Other leaders also brought troops to Outremer; Filangieri's southern Italian cavalry, Philip of Novara's mixed force and the Angevin king of southern Italy's French, Provençal and Catalan cavalry.

Wall-painting in the Templar Church at Cressac, western France, mid-late 12th century. (Author's photographs) Top: 'Crusaders emerge from their castle.' Below: Paintings on the lower register at Cressac are in a different, perhaps southern French, style.

Interior of the hall of the fortress and hospital at Aqua Bella (now Khirbat 'Iqbala) just west of Jerusalem, mid-12th century. (Photograph D. Pringle)

Following a series of Mamluk victories in the late-13th century, many families realized that there was no future in Syria or Palestine and so emigrated. Others fled when the final collapse came, but only those with money had this option. Many settled in Cyprus, since they no longer had connections in Western Europe, while others went to the Latin state of Greece. A few may even have gone to Cilician Armenia. In fact the numbers of knights in Cyprus increased dramatically as Crusader fortunes ebbed elsewhere, including *poulains* of mixed origin, several Armenian and Maronite colonies though not of noble rank. The Latin states of the Aegean were often short of troops, southern Greece having been conquered by a mere 100 knights and around 500 sergeants. Most came from Champagne and Burgundy, largely being of middle or lower ranking noble origin with a handful from the great baronial families. The Franco-Burgundian knightly aristocracy of Athens was then wiped out by the conquering Catalans in 1311. The Catalans themselves differed from previous settlers, the majority being light infantry with a small number of knights led by a highly educated élite which included the architect Ionnes Peralta. He repaired the dome of Santa Sofia in Constantinople following an earthquake in 1346. Meanwhile, all the Latin states of Outremer suffered the same desperate shortage of surviving male offspring, with many settler families dying out completely after only two generations.

After the Latin settlers in Greece lost most of the interior to Byzantine counter-attack they again became an urban coastal élite, a process reinforced by the arrival of Italian families who gradually came to dominate the French. In fact many of these Italian knights regarded their Greek fiefs as a form of financial investment while the chivalric society of the early 13th century gave way to one based upon trade. Of course not all newcomers were businessmen, 800 French knights invading northern Greece on behalf of the Angevins in 1331. Nevertheless it was the Italians who had the greatest influence. One way or another knights from a variety of backgrounds served in the armies of the southern Balkans.

The knights of the Aegean Crusader states seem to have been more willing to assimilate existing Slav military élites, and indeed to welcome Turkish settlers if they converted to Christianity, than the larger Greek military élite known as *archons*. But as the years passed and the Crusaders' shortage of manpower became acute, some *archons* were knighted and given hereditary fiefs despite remaining Orthodox Christians. To the north, in Epirus and Albania, the spread of Latin Christianity led to the emergence of two rival communities, the Catholic *Albanenses* and the Orthodox *Graeci*. During the 14th century the Albanian military élite was also feudalized, its forces included large numbers of light cavalry apparently led by local lords with the often unofficial status of knights.

Italian mercantile outposts in Outremer were largely defended by troops of Italian origin, in some cases assisted by locals. Most of the latter were Greek but in Malta, Gozo and Pantelleria the inhabitants were of Arab origin and many were still Muslim. Malta, in fact, served as a base from which the Italian corsair Enrico Pescatore attempted to conquer Crete at the start of the 13th century. Other pirates were also noblemen, Roland of Pisa being known as 'The Knight of Thessaloniki'. More famous was Licario, a poor knight from Vicenza who fled the Venetian island of Euboea following an unsuccessful love affair and entered Byzantine service in 1271. He then reconquered various Aegean islands for the Byzantine Emperor. Other pirate knights served Venice or Genoa, amongst the most successful being the Zaccaria brothers who controlled several ports along with the vital alum mines of the Anatolian coast, built a formidable fleet and in 1304 seized the wealthy island of Chios in the name of Genoa. The Crimean peninsula in the Black Sea was, however, the jewel of Genoese Outremer. Most of these little Genoese outposts were governed by associations of wealthy shipowners known as *mahonesi*, some of knightly rank, who won the support of local military élites by allowing them a share in their huge profits. Amongst these *mahonesi* were men of extraordinary geographical knowledge. Tedisio d'Orio of Kaffa in the Crimea was said to be interested in opening a trade route to China by travelling westwards, having learned what so many Arab geographers already knew – that the world was round a full 200 years before Christopher Columbus.

'Christ before Pilate'; wall-painting c. AD 1200 in the Hermitage of St Neophytos, Enkleistra. Though made when Cyprus was ruled by western Crusaders, the arms and armour of Pilate's guards are in purely Byzantine style.

ABOVE **Crac des Chevaliers (now Hisn al-Akrad) in western Syria was too expensive for the secular authorities to garrison and so was handed over to the Military Orders. (Author's photograph)**

'Crusaders massacre the Muslim population of Antioch'; *Universal History of William of Tyre,* **Acre, ad 1290-91. The leading knights carry oval shields characteristic of many troops during the final years of the Crusader states. (Bib. Laurenziana, Ms. Plut. LXI. 10, f.60v, Florence)**

One of the most notable characteristics of the knightly class of Outremer in the 13th and 14th centuries was their willingness to fight for a remarkable variety of leaders. The knights of Outremer, in fact, formed a pool of highly experienced mercenaries for the Catholic and Orthodox Christian armies of the Middle East and south-east Europe. The role of knights from Outremer in Muslim armies was naturally more controversial. A large number of troops from the Latin states in Syria and Palestine, including some knights, went over to Islam following the disastrous battle of Hattin in 1187 and there were also references to 'Frankish' troops fighting for the Ayyubids against rival Muslim rulers, some probably being mercenaries from the Latin states. A few members of the Latin élite also stayed following the collapse of the Crusader states, even holding fiefs under Mamluk overlordship for a decade or so. A much greater number of knights from Outremer and elsewhere certainly served in the Saljuq Turkish armies in Anatolia, even having their own *za'îm*, or leader, in the first half of the 13th century.

Motivation and pay

Religion was the main motivation behind the Crusades and the Church tried to maintain such fanaticism by proclaiming Muslims to be *summa culpabilis* – the 'most blameworthy' people. Even though religious motivation had declined by the 13th century a knight could win great prestige by serving in the Holy Land. A poem by Rutebeuf in praise of Geoffrey de Sergines, commander of the French Regiment in Acre, shows the mixture of religion and glory which motivated later 13th-century knights:

> *Before I could finish telling of his great valour and worth,*
> *His good breeding and good sense, it would be wearisome I think.*
> *He held his liege lord so dear that he went with him to avenge*
> *God's shame beyond the sea. Easily he will pay what he owes God,*

For he pays Him now every day at Jaffa where he rests,
If there is any rest in his warfare. There he wishes to use his time,
An ill neighbour and a terrible, and cruel and pitiless
The Saracens find him, for he never ceases to make war on them.

The knights of the Latin states in the Aegean were more down to earth in their motivation, many simply abandoning the Latin Emperor in Constantinople when he could no longer pay them. Several generations later the Catalan Grand Company which invaded Aegean Outremer found no difficulty in making long-term alliance with the Muslim Turks of this area. By the 1330s the Italian rulers of some Aegean states also became *illik kafirleri* or 'non-Muslim frontier lords' under Turkish suzerainty.

Although concepts of chivalry changed by the 13th century, war was not regarded as wicked but could be just, or even holy, the sin of fighting an unjust war falling on a leader, not his men. As far as the knights were concerned, the chivalric law of arms only served as a restraining principle if both sides agreed. Consequently, combat against non-Christians or non-noble infantry or in areas where the ancient code of vendetta took precedence over the newer concept of chivalry, could all degenerate into barbarism. Paradoxically knighthood itself had taken on a religious veneer; the old practice of a priest blessing a new knight's sword to protect it from the Devil having developed into a solemn dubbing ceremony. At the same time there were clear differences in the attitudes of north European knights and their southern (mediterranean) counterparts. These were reflected in Outremer where northern ideals predominated in earlier decades, southern in later years. Southerners rarely took knighting ceremonies and chivalric ideals so seriously, nor did they glorify warfare and the military life to the same extent. In urbanized Italy the 'girdle of knighthood' was even given to young men of bourgeois or working-class origin, provided their families were rich enough to provide the expensive equipment demanded of a cavalryman.

Nevertheless, social status remained important in the Crusader states, the 13th-century Kingdom of Jerusalem continually rewriting its laws to preserve a feudal structure which no longer had much meaning. Money was essential to the knightly élite whether serving as mercenaries or in a feudal array. A fief worth 900 to 1,000 *besants* a years was thought necessary to support a knight in the east, many being money fiefs. Yet knights could not always rely on income from fiefs or from employment as mercenaries, one report telling of an Italian who had to pawn his dagger, shield and armour, though notably not his sword and horse, when he fell into debt. Meanwhile, the system of *restor* meant that the King of Jerusalem paid for losses of horses or military equipment when his knights served outside the Kingdom. Pay varied considerably across Outremer but in general a

Donor figure and his horse on an *Icon of St Nicholas* from the Church of St Nicholas tis Steyis, Kalopetria, Crusader Kingdom of Cyprus, late 13th century. This knight is in purely western equipment while the front-only caparison of his horse is in a Mediterranean style associated with Italy and Spain. (Byzantine Museum, Archbishop Makarios III Foundation, Nicosia)

Book of Psalms, Acre or Antioch, late 13th century. 'King David plays his harp' and 'David beheads Goliath'. King David plays an unusual instrument with a handle at the top. Several eastern musical influences reached Western Europe via the Crusader states. (Bib. Antoniana, Ms. C.12, f.1v, Padua)

mercenary knight received twice or three times as much as a crossbowman, this reflecting the knight's superior status and the cost of his arms, armour and horses. *The Ordnance of Nicolas de Joinville* (1323-5) tried to fix the pay for cavalry in the Latin Principality of Achaia at 800 *hyperperes* for a year's service by a knight recruited overseas, 600 *hyperperes* if recruited locally, with 400 and 300 *hyperperes*, respectively, for squires.

Horses were the most expensive item that a knight needed. They were also amongst the most important booty, which in turn led to an infusion of superior oriental equine genes into European bloodstock. In the Crusader states, as elsewhere, different horses were used for different purposes, from *destrier* war-horses to the finest Turcoman travelling horses, ordinary *palfrey* riding horses, riding mules and *sumpters* or pack-horses. Courage and stamina were what a knight required of his war-horse, the innate aggression of stallions enabling them to ignore superficial wounds until a battle was over. Of course not all animals were of top quality, the mid-13th-century *Rule of the Templars* describing inferior horses as pullers, stoppers or throwers. *Destriers* were only ridden in battle, even then walking before cantering into the final charge. Trotting was so uncomfortable for an armoured man that it was commonly used as a form of punishment, while galloping would have broken up the close-packed *conrois* formation on which a knightly charge depended upon for its success.

Whereas the Latin states of Aegean Outremer lacked troops rather than horses, the Latin states of the Holy Land were not so fortunate. Here there was not only a shortage of remounts but also acute wastage in battle since Muslim horse-archers tried to unhorse their formidable foes. Prices varied hugely according to quality and availability. A good stallion was normally ten times the value of a mare, the best horses being twice as expensive again while the cost of a reasonable war-horse was around the same as a year's revenue from a normal fief.

Contrary to popular opinion, élite Muslim cavalrymen probably rode larger horses than those of the average Crusader. For this reason the best war-horses of 13th-century Western Europe were raised in areas which had close trading links with both Outremer and the Muslim world; for example Sicily and southern Italy, where improving breeds and exporting horses were major industries. The Latin states of the Aegean and of the Holy Land both imported great numbers of animals as well as high-usage items like horseshoes, the majority probably from southern Italy. Along with doctors and engineers which the Angevin rulers of this area sent eastward, there may have been vets since southern Italy was already producing some of the earliest European books on veterinary science. Where feeding was concerned, the Crusader states used whatever was available. This varied according to circumstance and an animal's feed-grain often contained so much debris that it had to be sieved. Grass and straw may, however, have been more nutritious than it sounds because medieval harvesting techniques left a great deal of grain in the fields.

EDUCATION AND TRAINING

In the Crusader Kingdom of Cyprus, elder sons from a knightly background were normally knighted when they reached 15, and were then expected to take part in military campaigns. This might sound young, but girls were bearing children from the age of fifteen or even thirteen. In 13th-century Western Europe and Outremer the education of boys from a knightly background started at five years of age. In one ide-alised description the child slept beneath an image of St Christopher. During the day he served his father, received religious instruction, learned to ride and played chequers. At seven years he left the care of women to become a page, learn the scientific but dangerous art of hunting and started to use weapons. Real military education began around the age of 12 once the child had some literacy, while for those of a higher rank Latin was also considered useful. Boys could be sent to the household of a great lord to complete their education; the sons of noblemen perhaps being sent to the ruler's court where they would not only be educated but would serve as hostages for their father's loyalty. At 14 a boy might become a valet and be put in charge of the hunting dogs as his first position of responsibility. At 20 he should be a fully qualified huntsman. A boy's education also emphasised good manners, clean-liness, singing, music and physical toughness. Once knighted, the young man was considered a *poursuivant* or 'learner', being encouraged to campaign further afield and broaden his experience.

Various literary sources shed light on the details of military training,

ABOVE **Ceramic plate showing a 13th century transport ship from Corinth. Such vessels provided a lifeline which enabled the isolated Latin states of Outremer to survive. (Corinth Museum; American School of Classical Studies photo-graph)**

BELOW **The ruins of a large medieval fortress overlooking Filipi in northern Greece. Many isolated towers dating from the Latin Crusader occupation are dotted across Greece, mostly in the south. (Author's photograph)**

Universal History of William of Tyre, Acre, late 13th century. (Bib. Munic., Ms. 562, Dijon) Top: 'Story of Troy.' The guard on the left has one of the earliest illustrations of a basilard dagger in western art. (f.89v) Below: 'Wooden Horse taken into Troy.' Infantry in the lower-right corner are representative of those troops who defended the Latin states in Syria during their final decades. (f.51r)

as when early 13th-century youngsters developed and displayed their strength by throwing weights and javelins. Individual jousting was called *bohordeis* and, at least in Outremer, men used lances of reed for training as their Muslim opponents did. Youths also tilted at the revolving *quintaine*. Although the late 13th-century *Rule of the Templars* was written for members of the Military Order, much of it reflects knightly practice. For example, hunting was not only a form of entertainment and military training but supplemented the food supply. Exercises carried out by the Military Orders would probably have been done by other knights of Outremer, though perhaps less enthusiastically. Three afternoons a week these included gymnastics, wrestling, a form of 'drill' which probably involved moving in formation with other mounted knights, and crossbow shooting, with prizes for marksmanship.

Horsemanship was not merely a matter of individual skill. All knightly training emphasised manoeuvring and charging in a tightly-packed *conrois* formation despite the horses' natural tendency to spread out when moving at speed. Such tactics involved riding stirrup to stirrup. A *conrois* formation normally consisted of from 20 to 40 riders in two or three ranks, a larger *conrois* perhaps being divided into *echelles* squadrons. These densely packed formations would only accelerate into a canter of 20 to 25 kilometres per hour during the final part of a charge. Nor would horses normally crash directly into other animals or field fortifications. In fact the impact of a knightly charge remained primarily psychological. The differences between these close-order western tactics and the more flexible tactics of their Muslim foes was reflected in Matthew Paris' description of an attempt by a group of Mamluks to enter Crusader-held Damietta while wearing captured equipment: 'But the nearer they approached the more unlike Frenchmen they seemed, for they marched hurriedly and in disordered crowds, and sloped their shields irregularly, more after the manner of Saracens than of French.'

Information from the Muslim side also sheds light on Crusader skills. For example, a late 13th-century training manual describes different ways of using a lance, amongst which was an individual charge down the left side of an opponent known as 'The Syrian Attack'. It was used by Christians and was, in effect, jousting. The Mamluk author noted, however, that it required a particularly high degree of nerve. Other Muslim accounts were less flattering; a description of a duel between a European mercenary and a Saljuq Turkish sultan around 1198 stated: 'The Frank descended upon him with his lance levelled. The sultan parried the blow with his shield and evaded a second attack. At the third pass he struck a terrible blow with his mace, surmounted by a bull's head, at the Frankish worshipper of the hoof of Jesus' donkey and he fell to earth. The Frank's horse had not been able to evade the mace-blow at its rider, who was solidly attached to the saddle and who now remained suspended, unconscious and senseless.'

Skill with the sword was equally important. Since early times Mediterranean warriors had clung to a Roman fencing tradition which emphasized thrusting rather than cutting. It influenced sword-play in Outremer and by the 14th century this more sophisticated 'Italian' fencing style also started to spread across Europe.

A specifically eastern form of cavalry training adopted in 13th-century Outremer was polo. Known as *chawgan* (bent stick) in Persian, *tschowgan* in the Caucasus and *tzykanion* in Byzantium, it eventually entered medieval French as *chicane*. Jousting by pairs of horsemen was of western origin but was soon recorded in Outremer; at Antioch in 1159, Cyprus in 1223 and the Kingdom of Jerusalem in 1286. A particularly famous and splendid tournament was held in the Isthmus of Corinth in Latin Greece in 1302 and lasted for twenty days. References to jousting 'in Catalan style' in 14th-century Sicily referred to the Moorish light cavalry tactics *á la jinete* used in Spain and probably also seen in the Catalan parts of Outremer.

The idea that medieval warfare relied on individual prowess with little forethought or planning is nonsense. In reality there was a science of war throughout the Middle Ages, with commanders relying on experienced soldiers and 'men of renown'. Ancient Greek and Roman military texts were translated, sometimes with attempts to update them for present conditions, but a leading Crusader commander like Oliver de Termes learned his skills in guerrilla-style war against the Albigensian Crusaders in

ABOVE 'The Road to Calvary,' on a marble tympanum from Larnaca, Cyprus, AD 1200-50. Two soldiers wear full mail-armour but no surcoats in a very rare piece of Crusader art from the first half of the 13th century. (V & A Museum, inv. A.2-1982, London; author's photograph)

BELOW South-western redoubt of Patras castle. The fortress is a mixture of Byzantine, Crusader, Venetian and Ottoman Turkish construction. (Photograph A. Bon)

southern France. Oliver was also renowned for the care he took of his men and his willingness to retreat without feeling guilty about it. Nevertheless the knights of Outremer were frequently lured, ambushed and surrounded by both Muslim and Byzantine foes. In 1291, even the Angevin king of southern Italy, Charles II, wrote that the Mamluks remained 'more clever and more adroit than Christians in war'.

SOCIETY AND CULTURE

The Latin élites retained an enormous sense of their own superiority over the indigenous peoples, giving them confidence long after their military dominance had been lost. Though there had been an increase in class consciousness amongst the aristocracy of Outremer since the later 12th century, the declining wealth of many knights made it difficult for them to marry outside the Crusader states. Consequently the Pope was often asked for special dispensation so that blood relatives could wed. Intermarriage with Orthodox Christians was resisted and in some cases banned. Punishments also reflected this rigid class structure; rebel knights in Venetian Crete losing their fiefs and non-noble Latins their assets, while Greeks lost a hand or foot.

The primary role of the knights of Outremer remained military, even though their way of life reflected that of urbanised Italy rather than rural France. In the Kingdom of Jerusalem the remaining rural fiefs were largely held by a city-based aristocracy whose representative gathered revenues from village leaders much as had been done before the Crusaders arrived. A similar system probably operated in Latin Cyprus and, to a lesser extent, Latin Greece. The castles and manors of Outremer varied considerably, recent detailed archaeological research having shown that there was no such thing as a specifically Crusader style castle. Here the way of life reflected that of southern Europe. The cellars were the

ABOVE RIGHT **Knightly tombs in the Crusader states were generally marked with incised slabs rather than three-dimensional effigies;**
A-B: **Members of the Lusignan family, late 13th century (Limassol Museum). C: Sir Reimont Doufour, late 13th/early 14th century. (Arab Ahmet Mosque, Nicosia). D: Raoul de la Blanchegarde, late 13th/early 14th century (Aya Sofia Mosque, Nicosia) E: Sir Balian Lanbert, d. AD 1337** (Armenian Church, Nicosia). F: **Sir Pierre Leiavne, d. AD 1300 (Arab Ahmet Mosque, Nicosia). G: Johan Tenouri, d. AD 1341 (Emerghieh Mosque, Nicosia). H: Sir Iaq d'Briess, early–mid 14th century (Aya Sofia Mosque, Nicosia). I: The Provost of Cyprus, mid-14th century (Emerghieh Mosque, Nicosia).** J: **Sir Phelipe de Milmars, mid-14th century (Emerghieh Mosque, Nicosia). K: Sibylle Creson, d. AD 1233, from the Kozan area (Archaeological Museum, Adana)**

main storage area for dried grain needed by people and animals, while the main hall above was used for ceremonies and feasts. Gates were often decorated as a mark of status and in 1252 the Count of Jaffa placed his coat of arms in every embrasure of his castle. A crude 13th-century carving of heraldic shields was, in fact, recently discovered in Crusader Ascalon.

Cyprus was not extensively fortified until a Mamluk naval threat grew serious later in the 14th century. A similar situation existed in the Duchy of Athens. At first the military élite of the Principality of Achaea tended to live in isolated mountaintop castles and strongly fortified manor-houses, until the rural interior was reconquered by the Byzantines. Finer examples of architectural decoration from Latin Greece show Islamic rather than Byzantine influence, suggesting that architects and masons as well as knights fled to Greece from the declining Crusader states of Syria and Palestine.

In the early days knights found that living amongst merchants and commoners in the crowded cities of Outremer caused social problems.

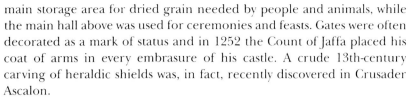

BELOW 'Tower of Babel', *Universal History of William of Tyre*, Acre, late-13th century. The labourers wear clothes in a mixture of western, Byzantine and Islamic styles while building techniques include a typical Middle Eastern mould for making unbaked mud-bricks. (Bib. Munic., Ms. 562, Dijon, f.9r)

The population of Crusader cities was, in fact, grouped by origin, not trade or class, each 'national' group having its own patron saint and church while the street-plans largely remained those which had existed for centuries. For example *balnea* bath-houses were merely the old Muslim *hammams*, the markets being unchanged while many churches had once been mosques. Many westerners believed that the Middle East promoted disease and that its heat and wine made men 'mad then dead'. Nevertheless, the élites of the Holy Land and Cyprus adopted several aspects of local diet and ways of coping with the climate.

The homes of wealthy families even in Cyprus resembled those of the Muslims, having a sort of private harem for the womenfolk. Little is known about houses in 13th-century Acre, but a remarkably detailed description of a comparable middle-class home in 12th-century Cairo survives in a document which reads like an estate agent's advertisement. This modest house filled part of a space between three streets. It had a main door and a 'secret door' off its enclosed courtyard, plus separate women's quarters and a cattle pen. Unlike a property across the street it did not have its own well or water wheel, but did include a kitchen and a wind-tower for ventilation. The front door was of fine wood, the entrance hall paved with marble and there were benches for visitors. Next came a corridor then two reception rooms facing each other, each with carved folding doors. One reception hall had carved wooden panelling, a large cabinet and the wind-catching ventilation tower with its own carved doors, plus a gilded wash-basin in front while the rest of the

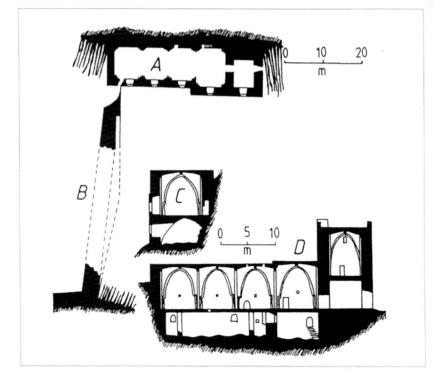

walls and floor were covered in marble and the ceiling was painted 'in oil according to the Syrian fashion'. A second reception room was similar except that its wash-basin was of multicoloured marble. The two covered sofas or benches were probably in these reception rooms. The courtyard had a marble fountain while the floor and walls were again panelled with marble. Small rooms led off this courtyard, each with carved wooden doors. The kitchen and a bathroom paved in marble and roofed with a carved plaster dome were also off the courtyard from which two balconies were reached by a stone staircase. Above was a carved plaster gallery, the upper floor being reached by a stone staircase in a small corridor. This upper floor consisted of three apartments, each with their own doors, wash-rooms and 'other facilities'. The roof had a parapet plus a wooden railing around the top of the staircase, while the house had its own rights to water from the city's canalisation system. If ordinary, knightly or middle-class houses in Acre were anything like this, then it is small wonder that European visitors were amazed by the apparent luxury of life in Outremer.

By the end of the 13th century there was considerable comfort even in castles, let alone the houses of the urban-based military élite, with carpets on the floors of the main rooms, flowery patterns painted on the walls and some rooms sprayed with eastern perfumes. Bathing was as much a source of pleasure as of cleanliness, which might explain the Church's distrust of this eastern habit. In Outremer singing and music-making formed an essential part of entertainment, while in Latin Greece the Greeks were shocked by the Latins' habit of drinking unwatered wine with their meals. Huge feasts were supposedly characteristic of the knightly way of life, but such indulgence was not an everyday thing, and by the end of the 13th century much of the refugee élite of Outremer was so poor that the Angevin king of southern Italy sent annual shipments of grain for the families of needy knights.

Where the costume of the knightly class was concerned there was less eastern influence than sometimes thought. Despite the fact that Willbrand of Oldenburg described the dress of the Latin élite of Cyprus as 'shabby' in 1211, rich oriental fabrics and minor aspects of eastern fashion were adopted during the 13th century. Large hats were used in high summer when, paradoxically, clothes seem to have been more western than in winter when fur-lined eastern mantles were worn. The Military Orders forbade luxurious items of costume as a threat to their puritanical code. These included pointed boots called *chausses avantpiés*, coloured coifs, whereas ordinary ones were white, and shoes called *galoches* as opposed to ordinary *soliers*. Other prohibitions from particular years included an embroiderd turban called a t*oaillon rechamé* which hung to the waist in 1262, long coats called *hargans* in 1288, a short *cote-hardie* coat with lacing points in 1300, and sandals called *planeaus* in 1302. In 1295 Members of the Hospitallers were, however, permitted to wear a white *oreillet* or *aureiller* form of head-covering which covers their ears. Meanwhile in Cyprus and Greece the Latin élite took pains to differentiate itself from the Greek majority, with laws supporting them in this effort, status being shown by wearing the symbols of knighthood, cloth-of-gold, spurs, sword and a sword-belt.

While the literature of Outremer naturally portrayed the Latin military élite in a favourable light, an interesting alternative exists in medieval Arabic literature. Here popular stories mock the westerners as stupid and primitive, the Crusaders being comparable to the Red Indians portrayed in old cowboy movies. European cities are described as exciting dens of vice, gambling and drunkenness like medieval versions of Las Vegas. Western men were portrayed as dirty, ignorant and promiscuous but also brave and strong, while western women were seen as no use for anything!

Religion remained the main divide between the military élites of Outremer and those they ruled, though many Latin settler families were eventually absorbed into Orthodox Christian Byzantine society. Before that, however, the 13th-century élites of Outremer followed the ideas of

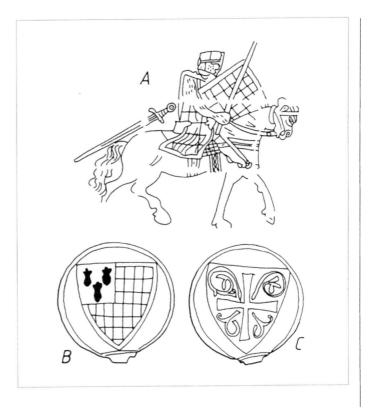

A series of windows in Chartres Cathedral portray leaders of St Louis' Crusade in 1250 where most of them were captured. Here (A) a nobleman bearing the arms of Dreux loses his sword – the only figure to do so. Some years ago an enamelled sword-pommel turned up in Damascus and is now in the Metropolitan Museum of Art, New York. On one side (B) it bears the blue and gold arms of Dreux quartered with the ermine of Brittany. On the other (C) it has a Crusader's red cross on a green ground decorated with vines. It is almost certainly the pommel of Count Peter's sword captured at al-Mansurah, but what was the forgotten story behind the sword on the stained-glass window?

Paris as closely as they could. Literature, wall-paintings and social events like tournaments all helped them to keep in touch with the latest fashions. The art and architecture of the Crusader states was, however, primitive compared to that of its sophisticated neighbours. Quite a lot of wall paintings survive while others were described in literary sources. The siege of Troy was a favoured theme in Crusader Greece, while the castle of St. Omer at Thebes was decorated with pictures of the Crusader conquest of Syria; its artists perhaps having come from Antioch itself with the Duke's wife. Though there were plenty of *troubadour* poets moving around Outremer, the question of original literary production is more difficult. For example, *The Old French Crusade Cycle*, based on legends associated with the First Crusade, probably contains sections written in Outremer. Stories about Ancient Greek heroes were also popular, particularly those involving battles against female Amazons. The same was true of the story of the Trojan War, while literature in Latin Greece was similar to that of French-dominated southern Italy, tales of King Arthur

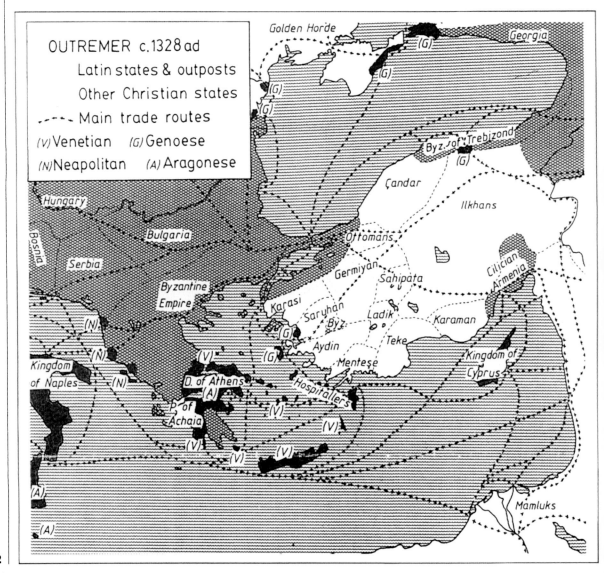

OUTREMER c.1328 ad
Latin states & outposts
Other Christian states
----- Main trade routes
(V) Venetian   (G) Genoese
(N) Neapolitan   (A) Aragonese

Chapel of Marqab castle, north-western Syria, late 12th/early 13th centuries, of black volcanic rock decorated with white limestone. The best domestic buildings in the Principality of Antioch were probably made in the same manner.

being very popular. Not until the 14th century did Italian challenge French as the language of the élite in Latin Greece.

The ideal of courtly love also began to appear in 13th-century literature, encouraged by ladies and their minstrels. It was based upon Arab-Muslim concepts of romance, as opposed to the old Graeco-Roman emphasis on sexual appetite. Gradually it changed the women of the knightly class from valuable possessions or vehicles for political alliances almost into equals of their menfolk. Meanwhile the ideals of knightly behaviour came to include the enthusiastic pursuit of sexual favours. Strangely enough the Templars came to play a prominent role in literary romance. The reasons are complex but perhaps the Templars' connection with 'Solomon's Palace' in Jerusalem (actually the al-Aqsa Mosque) contributed to the idea, King Solomon having himself had a formidable reputation as a lover.

ON CAMPAIGN

During the 13th century the military establishment of the Crusader States was dominated by the Military Orders, Italian merchant communes and the urban bourgeosie. Nevertheless the old officers of state played a prominent role for as long as royal authority survived. For the knights, the most important officer was the *sénéchal* in charge of castles and of the *bailis* or rulers' military representatives. He could change garrisons but not the *chatelains* in command. Next came the *connétable* army commander who organised military formations, allocated duties, checked men's competence and kit and had primary responsibility for the knights. The *maréchal* second-in-command organised the army, recruited mercenaries, checked their equipment and organised supplies including horses and baggage animals. The *maréchal* was also responsible for discipline, though he was not per-mitted to strike anyone of knightly rank. The five *grand sergeants* or main officers of state in Crusader Cyprus were similar. A comparable military structure existed in Aegean Outremer where, however, the feudal hierarchy was simpler than in Western Europe. Things changed when the Duchy of Athens fell under Catalan rule; the main officers now being a political *vicar general* and a military *marshal* who was always selected from the knights of the Catalan Grand Company. After the Catalans accepted the overlordship of the Aragonese king of Sicily each district had its own political *veguer* (vicar) and military *castellano* or captain.

'King Ninus and his Retinue', Universal History of William of Tyre, Acre, late 13th century. (Bib. Munic., Ms. 562, Dijon, f.14r)

23

Icon of St Sergius, late 13th century, Crusader states. While the Saint is portrayed as a light cavalry *turcopole*, the donor is a Latin woman wearing the long black veil adopted by the ladies of Outremer. (St Catherine's Monastery, Sinai)

Military obligations were basically the same across Outremer, with few local variations. In the Kingdom of Jerusalem a knight was expected to serve until he reached 60, though he could send a deputy after the age of 40. He might, however, have been excused duty in defence of a city wall which was widely seen as beneath his dignity. By the 13th century there was also greater variation in the quality of equipment than was seen in Western Europe. Knights could be summoned even if they only had one sickly horse, though they could ask their lord for a spare. Feudal service in Syria, Palestine and Cyprus could be for the full year if it remained within the state, but fell to four months when campaigning outside. According to the feudal legal code of Aegean Outremer, a knight's service involved four months in a castle garrison, four guarding the frontier, and four at home as an emergency reserve, while military obligations in the Italian mercantile outposts mirrored those in their mother cities.

Garrison service must have been tedious and the food could be poor. On the other hand the strength of medieval fortification largely depended on the quantity and quality of its provisions of wheat, wine, iron, steel and leather. During the day gates were normally guarded by knights or comparable men-at-arms and were probably shut at compline, the last religious service of the day. Knights formed just over a third of the cavalry in most castles of Outremer, horsemen being about a third of the total fighting force which was in turn around a quarter of the total inhabitants. Some Italian trading outposts of Outremer were defended by remarkably garrisons, though the most important Genoese settlements did have their own military *baylia* in charge of defence.

The Crusader proverb that 'a castle destroyed was a castle half built' did not help when Outremer was so desperately short of troops. In many cases a small enemy force could blockade a Latin castle – a handful of attackers watching a handful of defenders. Knights of the Crusader Kingdom of Jerusalem were theoretically excused combat on foot during siege warfare but in reality they played a prominent role; for example, defending siege-engines from enemy raids at night. A poem by the early 13th-century French poet Bernat Arnaut de Moncuc betrays his delight in siege warfare and there is no reason to suppose attitudes were different in Outremer:

> An armoured horse, a hauberk, a polished lance, a good steel blade.
>   I take pleasure in seeing archers near the loopholes,
> When the stone-throwers shoot and the wall loses its parapet,
>   And when the army grows in numbers,
> And forms ordered ranks in many an orchard.

The knights of Outremer were also involved in ravaging enemy territory or trying to ambush enemy raids. Here the main role of knightly cavalry was to protect their infantry, guard baggage and booty, carry out reconnaissance, cut enemy communications and seize their supplies. Although the knightly charge remained the main offensive tactic available to a Crusader commander, more often than not the Latins merely reacted to their opponents' movements rather than seizing the initiative. The knights were also highly vulnerable if a charge failed to hit its target, often themselves being struck in the flanks or rear.

Whereas the Mamluks followed a concerted strategy aimed at undermining the Latin states and spanning several generations, most Crusader raids were merely short-term political gestures. Even so the raiders usually spent some days in their target area. They also tended to capture rather than kill the enemy and as a result the Crusader states soon possessed a large number of Muslim slaves. Targets for such *chevauchées* ranged from terrorizing small frontier villages to the destruction of cultural targets such as holy sites.

As the years passed the role of heavy cavalry declined in Outremer while that of infantry and mounted crossbowmen rose. The knights did, however, have the advantage of being much quicker to muster. *The Rule of the Templars* described the mustering of knights in detail, and things would have been similar when assembling secular knights. At the start of a campaign they were summoned from their quarters with their horses, pack animals and livestock for food. In camp their squires found and fetched water and fuel, though they were not allowed beyond earshot. The designated *gonfanonier* standard-bearer and his assistants called out orders, distributed fodder and commanded the squires. Other 13th-century sources indicate that knightly households had their own war cry. Knights also shaved and cut their hair before a campaign to provide a better fit for their helmets and to show respect for their foes. Discipline could be fierce and even the taking away of a knight's sword-belt was humiliating for a member of this proud military élite. Punishments varied upon one's status. Thus a mercenary knight who broke his contract could have his entire armour confiscated, while an ordinary soldier had his hand pierced with a hot iron.

On the line of march knights rode in front with their squires being in charge of their lances, shields and war-horses. Next came the baggage. In a peacetime march men were permitted to water their horses at streams, but in war they could only do so when and where the gonfanonier stated. The most experienced knights were placed at the front and rear, and in the Crusader states these tended to be members of the Military Orders.

History of Outremer, French early 14th century. (Bib. Nat., Ms. Fr. 9081, Paris) TOP **A man is murdered while playing backgammon, a game popular with the knightly élite. (f.160r)** ABOVE **Religious and fealty formalities, including the ceremonial handing over of a glove by a ruler. (f.174)**

Tents were varied, simple ridge types appearing as early as the 9th century, plain and highly decorated bell tents becoming common in the late 12th century, large pavilions being seen from the late 13th century onwards. Not surprisingly the Crusaders came into contact with both the Arab and Turkish tent traditions as well as the often magnificent structures used by the Islamic military élites. Nevertheless the basic structure of 13th-century tents consisted of canvas with ropes sewn into the seams. Grommets at the eaves were knotted through leather tabs, cord latcheting being used to attach wall cloths while the eaves had valances and skirtings. Tent poles seem to have been topped with 'spindles' or spikes passing through an 'onion' or reinforced pad at the peak. These were then surmounted by a 'dolly' or 'vase'.

Naval warfare

During the 13th and 14th centuries naval warfare became more important for the scattered outposts of Outremer than campaigns on land. But raiding was usually on a small scale with the military aristocracy engaging in little more than piracy. Most of the marines aboard Angevin galleys were mailed knights recruited in Provence, but they proved less agile than their non-noble lightly armoured Catalan *almogavar* rivals. The crews of ships manned by Latin settlers in 14th-century Aegean Outremer, especially those of the Venetian colonies, were summoned by a public crier a week before sailing, then again on the day of departure, being fined if they did not turn up properly armed. Such maritime expeditions involved considerable hardship even for the knights, the basic food being hard biscuit, though

The fortified peninsula of Skopa in Kotronas bay in southern Greece, an ideal position for a garrison depending on Italian control of the sea. (Photograph A. Bon)

figs and wine could be purchased along the way. In winter the fragile war-galleys were taken out of the water, placed under cover and guarded by a local garrison. It is also worth noting that galley-slaves had not been used since the fall of the Roman Empire. Byzantine and Muslim navies remained volunteers except for the personal servants of senior officers throughout the Middle Ages and it was the Hospitallers of Rhodes who reintroduced galley-slaves or, more accurately, 'galley-serfs' to the Mediterranean.

At sea crossbowmen formed the main defence while marines, including knights, attempted to board enemy vessels. Knights were more important in the naval landings which often involved *taridas*, a specialised horse-transporting galley of Arab origin in which the animals stood in stalls down the centre of the vessel. By using its oars a *tarida* could back on to a beach and disgorge its troops directly into battle like modern landing craft. Meanwhile, larger ships stood offshore, unloading their cargoes of men, horses and supplies into small boats. One mid-12th century account described such a descent upon an enemy coast: 'First the archers disembarked, each with his bow bent, his quiver and bowcase hanging at his side, the knights disembarking and forming up on shore once the beach was secure.' Occasionally fully armoured knights attacked the enemy first, though whether they rode out of their ships or led their horses into the shallows remains a mystery. Given the size of medieval Mediterranean ships it is more likely to have been the latter.

Battle and it's aftermath

Although full-scale battles formed a minor part of warfare in Outremer, they are often described in detail. Leaders strengthened the morale of those involved with pre-battle speeches. The knights formed up behind their *conrois* banners and once fighting started they listened for the trumpets which were used to restore order, rally or summon troops. Whether knights were more fearful of close combat with other cavalry or of arrows is unknown, but the former probably caused more horrific wounds and fatalities. Scientific evidence shows that crossbows and even

Icon of St George, 13th century, Latin state of Greece, reflecting the mixed military styles which developed in Aegean Outremer. (Inv. 89, Byzantine Museum, Athens; author's photograph)

the feared composite bows of Muslim horse-archers normally had to be shot from close range to penetrate armour to any great depth.

The primary function of the mounted knights in their closely packed *conrois* formations was to break the enemy line then turn and charge again. By the 13th century repeated charges by successive divisions plus reserves was the favoured tactic, though Muslim forces rarely provided a static target for multiple charges. On the contrary they attempted to lure a Crusader cavalry charge so as to tire their enemy, disrupt his formations and ambush any unit that made itself vulnerable. The knights of the Latin Aegean states had similar tactical problems, particularly when they were faced by armies which included Turco-Mongol horse archers.

Once again the mid-13th-century *Rule of the Templars* explains what a knight was supposed to do in case of a setback. If unable to rally to his own leader's banner he should make for the marshal's banner or that of any other Christian leader. Only if all banners fell should he flee. The part-Byzantine, part-Latin prince Theodore Paleaologus writing in 1326 advised that if a force was caught unawares the fighting men should not try to form separate units but should quickly gather into a single body while the squires and pack animals drew up a short distance to the rear where they could collect and guard any prisoners and secure riderless horses.

Knights were often used to strengthen foot soldiers. The English Crusader King, Richard the Lionheart is also credited with the tactical innovation of drawing up infantry with a front rank of men using their spears as pikes and their large shields as pavises, thus protecting a crossbowman and loader who stood behind each two shield-bearers; the whole formation being stiffened by armoured knights. In fact Richard probably learned this idea in the Middle East where it had been a normal infantry formation for centuries. Another possible example of Middle Eastern tactical influence was the placing of knightly cavalry within a protective infantry box.

The traditional ethos of knightly behaviour emphasised prowess in individual combat while Muslim tactics and, to a lesser extent, those of Byzantine south-eastern Europe emphasised harrassment, with close combat used when an enemy had been softened up or caught by surprise. One ambush in southern Palestine in 1192 was described in detail by the chroniclers of both sides. It involved Arabs and Turks using arrows and javelins at short range, wreaking havoc amongst the Crusaders' horses. In the resulting mélée men with inferior armour were easily killed while those better protected were knocked senseless by many blows. Other men were thrown from their horses then protected by a circle of friends as they remounted. The French Crusader De Joinville

was similarly struck by arrows five times, his horse no less than 15, at the battle of al-Mansurah. He was also thrown from his horse but lay beneath his shield as the enemy rode over. Even in the 13th and 14th centuries knights were highly vulnerable to more nimble foot soldiers if unhorsed.

There are plenty of detailed descriptions of duels even during a larger battle. In the *chansons de geste* knights attempted to drag their opponents from their saddles by grasping their helmets and individuals could also be pinned to the wooden frame of their saddles by a lance through the leg. De Joinville was pinned to his horse's neck by a spear-thrust in 1250. Unable to draw his sword from its scabbard he used a second blade slung from his saddle. Some decades later a captured Catalan *almogavar* infantryman was pitted against a fully armoured Angevin knight in Latin Greece. The unarmoured *almogavar*, armed with a spear, light javelin and light sword, awaited the horseman's charge then at the last moment threw his javelin into the horse's chest and dodged the rider's lance. As the knight tumbled from his wounded horse the Catalan cut his helmet thongs and held his sword at the Angevin's throat. The captive *almogavar* was then given fine clothes and set free. In an early 13th-century *chanson de geste* a knightly hero uses six of his seven available shields in combat with men and beasts. Elsewhere heavy blows made the *enarmes*, or holding straps, break free from a shield, while in the late 12th-century story *Elioxe*, men abandoned their helmets and threw the coifs off their heads as they fled.

The fate of the wounded could be grim. Battles often culminated in hand-to-hand brawling in which heavy armour was more of a hindrance than a help. Literary and archaeological evidence both show that medieval weapons tended to incapacitate rather than kill outright. Other early 13th-century sources describe wounded knights carried from battle on litters so that they could be treated. In medical terms Western Europe was less advanced than Byzantium or the Muslim countries, but battlefield surgery in Outremer was surely influenced by its neighbours. In fact Jerusalem had become a medical teaching centre before its recapture by Saladin in 1187. Here vinegar and lead oxide were used as antiseptics for superficial wounds while both Jewish and Muslim physicians were highly regarded throughout Outremer, despite Church disapproval.

The Arsenal Bible, Acre, late 13th century, perhaps the most Byzantine-influenced manuscript from the Crusader states. (Ms. Ars. 5211, Bib. de l'Arsenal, Paris) LEFT 'The Army of Holofernes.' (f.330) RIGHT 'Pharoah's army in the Red Sea.' (f.293)

ARMS AND ARMOUR

Since there was virtually no arms industry in Outremer almost all military equipment had to be imported from Western Europe, the only other source being captured enemy material. On the other hand the perishable wooden, leather or fabric parts of arms and armour were made locally, certainly in the Latin Aegean and possibly also in the Latin states of the Holy Land. For example, the Angevin ruler of Naples established a local armoury in the Greek castle of Clarence in 1281, whereas previously even arrowheads had to be sent from Italy. A local armourer in Crete similarly manufactured *curacijs* body-armours in 1336.

The bulk of arms and armour came from Italy which had been a major centre of production since at least the 12th century, Genoa being the main centre of export. Most of the armours sent to Outremer and Byzantium in the late 12th century were mail hauberks, but in 1205 the Genoese intercepted a Venetian ship carrying no less than 1,200 shields, plus other weapons. Items of armour mentioned in Italian trading

records also included equipment that was rented rather than sold, consisting of the *barberia* (coif), *osbergum* (hauberk), *corellus* (cuirass) and *panceria* form of hauberk. Meanwhile Genoa also imported fine quality steel blades from the Muslim countries of the east, apparently camouflaging them as 'spices' in its commercial records before reselling them elsewhere. During the 14th century Albania and Epirus similarly imported large amounts of arms from Italy. One way or another there was plenty of military equipment moving around Outremer.

Mail gave relatively little protection from missiles shot at close range and the Crusaders must soon have realized that metal or even hardened leather lamellar armour, such as that used by many Middle Eastern troops, was more effective. The late 13th century was certainly a period of considerable experimentation in the use of many different materials, though this may have started much earlier. Materials included whalebone, horn, *cuir-bouilli* (hardened leather), *latten* which was similar to brass, and steel. Textile and leather-workers were also involved in the armour business, particularly where padded 'soft armour' was concerned. While buff leather was probably used for straps, *cuir bouilli* was widely used as a lighter alternative to iron. It was not 'boiled leather', which would simply have been soft, but had been shaped and hardened by a method similar to modern blocking. In this process oil softens the leather before shaping, though the leather might also have been softened by prolonged immersion in cold water. Hardening was done by heating and drying in moulds. The term *bouilli* possibly came from *boulue* which was itself a surface waterproofing process using molten wax.

Medieval plate-armour so far analysed chemically was not cold-worked merely by hammering and shaping. Instead, a study of its ferrite grains shows that the iron was heated then beaten into shape. One 14th-century great helm was of mild steel worked at over 500 degrees centigrade, though the great majority of pre 15th-century armour was of softer iron. Plates varied in thickness from 3mm for the front of a helmet, to 2mm for a breastplate and a mere 1mm for arms and leg defences. Nevertheless experiments have shown that such plate-armour protected its wearer from fatal injuries even at short range, though not from disabling wounds. Another experiment indicates that the manufacture of a medieval sword took about 200 man-hours while a full mail hauberk plus *chausses* required several weeks. Such statistics were reflected in the consistently high price of good quality arms while the fact that Outremer imported virtually all its gear must have added to its expense.

Changes in the arming of a knight reflected changes in his armour. The following description of a southern French knight equipping himself for battle, written by Arnaut Guilham de Marsan in the late 12th century, would also have applied to a knight of Outremer:

TOP **The Main chapel of Crac des Chevaliers was originally decorated with wall paintings, fragments of which survive. (Syrian Dept. of Antiquities photograph)** ABOVE **Small donor figure in a wall-painting from Crac des Chevaliers. His clothing appears to be looser than that normally worn in Europe. (Archaeological Museum, Tartus; Syrian Dept. of Antiquities photograph)**

Wall painting, 14th century, possibly showing 'The child Jesus being presented at the Temple.' The arms & armour include Byzantine influence and might reflect the equipment used in the Crusader states of Greece. (In situ, the Cathedral, Salerno; author's photograph)

'I have a good war-horse and I will tell you what kind; one that is swift running and suitable for arms. Take this one at once, and then your armour, lance and sword and hauberk with its surcoat. Let the horse be well tested and not an inferior one; and put on it a good saddle and bridle and a really good peytral [breast-strap securing the saddle] so that nothing is unsuitable, and have the saddle-cloth made with the same emblem as the saddle and the same colour as is painted on the shield, and the pennon on the lance in the same way. Have a pack-horse to carry your doubled hauberk and your weapons held high so that they appear more splendid, and always have the squires close by you.'

Late 12th-century poems from Outremer such as *Les Chetifs* also mention a *clavain* neck-armour which was probably quilted. It, like the mail *chausses* protecting the legs, was put on before the hauberk. Then came the sword, sword-belt, *mesericorde* dagger which become popular in Outremer before western Europe, and finally a shield and lance. These verses indicate that the mail coif and *ventail* were still part of the hauberk, and that the coif included leather lining and probably integral padding. The similarly dated Crusader poem *Beatrix* adds further details, referring to shields with bosses, helmets made of four 'quarters', *chausses* being laced to the legs, a *turciosed* (Turcified) coif which almost certainly meant that it was padded and given a decorative cloth. There were also saddles with ivory decoration and felt padding plus rich fabric *couvertures* for the horses. The knight was then advised to check that his feet were firmly in his stirrups, which was not surprising when a 12th- to 14th-century hauberk weighed around 25 kilograms. On the other hand modern experiments show that such armour was neither tiring nor uncomfortable even in hot weather. Certain decorative elements also began to appear in later 12th-century *chansons de geste*, including the surcoat and a cloth *volet* or 'veil' tied around the helmet.

The Rule of the Templars again provides detailed information for 13th-century Outremer. Here the knight's equipment was a hauberk, iron *chausses*, helmet or lighter war-hat, *espalière* for the shoulders, *solerets* for the feet, padded *jupeau d'armer* (from the Turco-Arabic *jubbah* quilted armour) to be worn beneath the hauberk, *ecu* shield, lance, sword, 'Turkish mace', and *couteau d'armes* dagger. The rest of the kit was a dagger, a knife for bread, a third small knife, two shirts, two pairs of breeches, two pairs of hose, a small belt for his shirt, a small sack for his nightshirt, another small sack for his quilted soft-armour, a leather sack

Arms and armour, c. AD 1190 (See text commentary for detailed captions)

A

Conroi's training, c. AD 1200

B

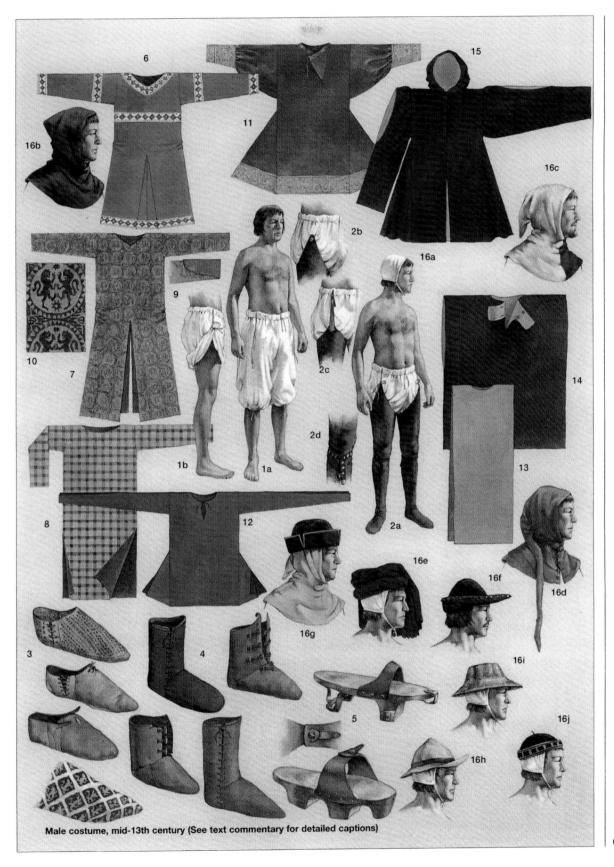

Male costume, mid-13th century (See text commentary for detailed captions)

C

Battle of Nicosia, Cyprus, AD 1229

D

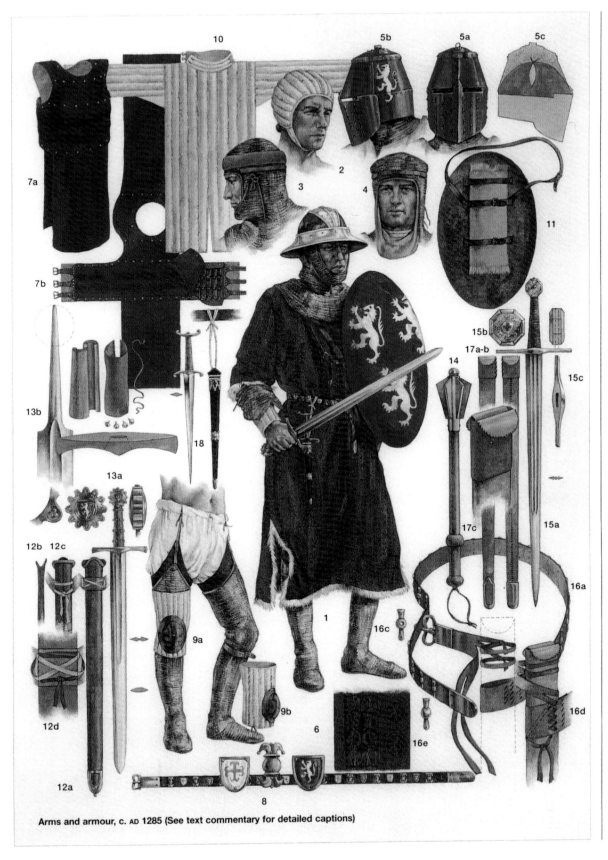

Arms and armour, c. AD 1285 (See text commentary for detailed captions)

E

Capture of the Minbar from the mosque at Nablus, AD 1242

F

Sugar factory-fief, c. AD 1280

G

3a

3b

4a

3c

3d

3e

5

1

2

3f

3g

Horse harness, early 13th/ mid-14th century

Tournament on Isthmus of Corinth, AD 1302

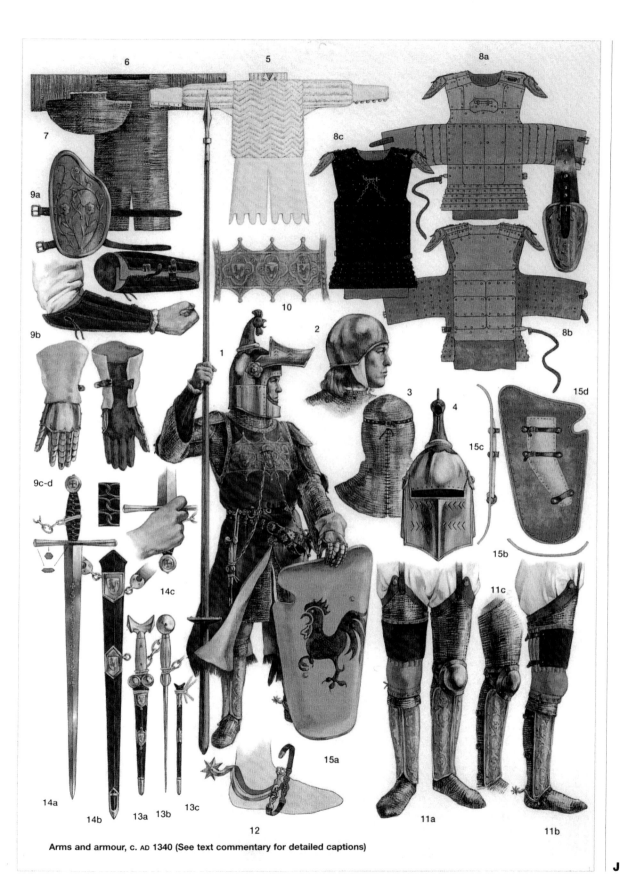

Arms and armour, c. AD 1340 (See text commentary for detailed captions)

for his hauberk, a hat and a felt bonnet. The armour of Outremer was also described by its enemies, notably in the mid 13th-century Turkish Danishmandnamah epic:

His armour and his harness were complete,
All his body and the chest of his horse were covered in iron.
His saddle and the scabbard of his sword were of gold,
And on his chest he hung an idol [probably a crucifix].
He took his lance in his hand, this horseman,
And quickly threw himself upon Melik [the Turkish hero].

Various forms of padded protection could also be worn alone, sometimes because a wounded man could not bear the weight of mail. Changes coming into fashion in the later 13th century are better described in Italian sources than in those from Outremer. In 1260, for example, a central Italian mercenary was expected to present himself in full knightly gear consisting of either a mail *pansière* or hauberk, *stivaletti* mail *chausses*, a brimmed war-hat, cuirass or *lamières* early forms of plate-armour, lance and a shield of either the *ecu*, *targe* or larger *tavolaccio* type. Seventeen years later a surviving mercenary contract demands a good war horse, good armour with either *panzeria et harneriis* or *coraziniis* of

perpunto grosso et conscialibus ferreis (quilted with iron lining, probably of scales), *gamberuolis* or *calicas ferreis* leg defences, *gorgiera* for the neck, *elmo ferreis* or *bascinetto* helmets, *scuto* or *tavolaccio* shields, plus sword, dagger and lance. In 1283 even a non-élite cavalryman in the rich Angevin army had a *cervelière* light helmet, *epaulière* shoulder armour, and iron *gorgière* to protect the neck, plus a sword and *couteau* dagger. Another mercenary contract from Bologna, dated 1296, insisted that knightly cavalry ride armoured horses and have *panceriam* and *cassettum* body-armour, a large helmet with *manicis cirotecas de ferro* arm defences, *ferro gamberias* or *schinerias* for their legs, *sovosbergani* or *lamerias* with *faldis spontonem* for the trunk and abdomen, *capello de ferro* or *bacilletum* light helmets with *capirone de ferro* or *barbata* coifs or *aventails*, *clipeum* or larger *tabolatum magnum* shields, *lanceam* lance, *spatam* sword and *cultellum de ferro* iron dagger. Virtually the same would have been used by the best equipped knights of late 13th-century Outremer.

Descriptions from the 14th century are more varied, with for example, slight differences when preparing for a tournament or a battle. In both cases a brazier was supposedly lit and a carpet laid before the knight stripped to his shirt and combed his hair. For a tournament he put on leather shoes or leggings. Over these came plates of steel or *cuir bouilli* to protect his thighs, knees and calves. Next came the quilted *aketon* then a mail hauberk and coif; a cuirass or an unspecified form of 'leather hauberk', a surcoat with the knight's coat-of-arms, and his whalebone gauntlets. Lastly he put on his sword-belt and helmet. For war an iron *plates de alemayne* cuirass and *gorgières* neck defences were added, while for jousting an *aketon*, hauberk and *gambeson* with a fine outer layer of the best silk, plus steel plates or cuirass, shield, *bascinet* and great helm were advised.

In Mediterranean areas like Outremer hardened leather armour persisted

longer than it did in the colder north. Once again surviving Italian documents provide detailed information which would also apply to Outremer. An early 14th-century professional cavalryman was expected to have a saddle, horse armour, *panzeriam* or *asgergum* mail body-armour, *caligas* boots or greaves or iron *stivalettos*, *cappelum de acciario* war hat, *lamerias vel coraczas* coat-of-plates, lance and a shield of either the *scutum*, *targiam* or *tabolaccium amplum* type. The lighter arms also popular in Aegean Outremer are mirrored in the military treatise written by Theodore Paleaologus:

'Indeed in the matter of mounted soldiers... each with his armour and equipment, he should have two small horses like those of the Greeks and the Turks, that is to say geldings, or at least two mares, and that he be armed to match the strength of his horses. That is to say with doublet, *haubergeon* and gorgeret, cuirass and *gambeson*, chapel de fer, sword of one type or another at his side, greaves and *cuisses* and his lance and shield. And if he wishes to have great horses, that is to say destriers in Latin style, let him be armed with heavy armour suitable for that purpose.... And in this connection let their surcoats be provided with a badge like that on their banners, ensigns and the pennons of their lances to make a good show of their people, and this I would also apply to mounted lesser people of the said districts. Vassals and knights should have three horses, a destrier, a good palfrey and a good packhorse to carry their necessary equipment. Barons and those of higher rank should each have at least five horses with their harness, and each should have a good squire

The largely 13th-century Kiz Kalesi fortress on an islet opposite the fortified port of Le Courc (now Korikos) on the coast of Cilicia. (Author's photograph)

LEFT Icon of St George and the Young Man of Mitylene, possibly made at Lydda in the Kingdom of Jerusalem, mid 13th century. Although the saint wears unrealistic pseudo-Roman armour he rides a horse with a realistic 13th-century saddle. (National Icon Collection, no. 13, British Museum, London)

to keep him company by his side, and none of them should spare expense for in bearing himself well it turns to his honour and profit, and his renoun is increased.'

Soft-armour had always been worn beneath mail and may have been of felt in the early days. The quilted *aketon* and *gambeson* soft-armour probably reached Europe in the 12th century from the Middle East via the Crusades. They were thick enough to make their wearer appear conspicuously bulky, though late 13th-century evidence shows that most of the padding was at the front. The *clavain* neck and shoulder protection may have also originally been quilted. The 13th-century shoulder-covering *spaulder* was similarly made, though by 1302 a comparable *espalière de balainne* incorporated pieces of whalebone.

Mail was worn with its rivet-heads outermost to avoid chaffing and in Europe it was usually made of alternating solid and riveted links. Experiments have shown that a long mail hauberk tended to wrap around a rider's legs but no adequate explanation has yet been found for the 'doubled' hauberks so often mentioned in both European and Islamic sources. Perhaps it simply meant wearing two armours. With the separation of mail coifs from hauberks in the 13th century and the widespread replacement of coifs with mail *aventail*s attached to the rims of helmets in the 14th century, the raised collars of hauberks were clearly stiffened and padded. The 14th century also saw greater use of the short-sleeved *haubergeon* worn with rigid arm-defences. The *panceriam* remains a mystery, though the will of Barzella Merxadrus of Bologna who died on Crusade at Damietta 1219-20 stated:

'To the Hospital of the Germans, where he wishes to be buried, he left all his arms and armour and his panceriam with one long sleeve and coif.'

Casigans in Crusader documents are more easily explained; these simply being *kazaghand*, padded and cloth-covered mail armours captured in battle or copied from the Muslims.

Simple forms of plate-armour were used at an earlier date than is gen-

47

Seal of John II d'Ibelin, Lord of Beirut, AD 1260, from Santa Maria dei Teutonici, Venice. The leader of one of the most powerful Crusader families in the east is shown in complete European arms and armour. (Inv. b.3, n.55, Archivio di Stato, Venice)

erally realized. Early versions of the *cuirie* or *quiret* were probably buff leather, possibly lined and padded, and were mentioned from the late 12th century onwards. By the 14th century they were rigid enough to serve as anchor points for guard-chains to the sword, ensuring that a knight did not lose his weapon in battle. The *curie* came in various styles: side lacing or with shoulder buckles or simply slipped over the head. The late 13th–early 14th–century cuirass or pair of cuirasses was at first similar to the *cuirie*, consisting of two pieces of hardened leather though they may have also included internal plates or scales. Body-armour of vertical plates or splints was, however, known in late 13th-century Germany. Some surviving cuirasses from the second quarter of the 14th century are made of solid horizontal iron hoops, these presumably having replaced the earlier vertical splints. A larger plate for the middle of the chest appeared in the mid 14th century, eventually evolving in the breast-plate.

Meanwhile, in areas influenced by Italy the late 13th-century *corazza* seems to have had features in common with the Islamic or Byzantine leather lamellar *jawshan*. During the 14th century the more widely known coat-of-plates evolved out of the earlier pair of plates, hauberk of plates or simply plates. While early forms of cuirass proved effective against lances, arrows and cutting swords, they were less effective against the thrusting style of fencing which came into use in the mid 13th century. Cuirasses of this type had two or three rows of internal plates or splints protecting the body but were regarded as old-fashioned by the mid 14th century. The brigandine was a more flexible form of cuirass consisting of much smaller plates, first being mentioned around 1367 – again in Italy.

Additional protection for the arms began to be seen in the late 12th century, first as mail mufflers or mittens for the hand. Fingered mittens appeared later in the 13th century but started to die out after 1330. By then separate gauntlets were common, having first appeared in the late 13th century as mail-covered gloves. Next came whalebone between layers of fabric or leather, then metal scales which were increased in size but reduced in number from 1340 onwards. *Ailettes* attached to the shoulders were solely for heraldic display, the first rigid protection for the arms being disc-shaped *besagews* laced to the outside of the elbow. They were seen from around 1260, being replaced by shaped *couters* covering the outside of the elbows in the mid 14th century. Tube-like protections for the arms are likely to have reflected Islamic or Byzantine styles, themselves perhaps reflecting Sino-Mongol military influence. The earliest known European reference to such armour was in a document of around 1260-70 by Rusticiano of Pisa. In 1302 a *bras de fer* appears in a French source; almost certainly being an early *rerebrace* for the upper arm. By 1330 full armour for the arm consisted of a *vambrace* (lower arm), couter (elbow), *rerebrace* (upper arm) and spaulder (shoulder). The latter may first have been seen in Italy around 1340 and often appears to be made of hardened leather.

Leg protections developed earlier than separate arm defences,

perhaps never having entirely died out since the fall of the Roman Empire. Mail *chausses* sometimes covered the entire leg while others consisted of a mail strip down the front. References in the Crusade Cycle poem *Les Chetifs* to iron *chausses* being 'white like flowers in a meadow' suggests that in Outremer such protections could be covered in decorative cloth in Islamic style. Another similarly dated French *chanson de geste* refers to padded or quilted *chauces ganbaisiées*. Other forms of leg protection only appeared in the 13th century, though there is also an interesting reference to *genellières* which 'hung like window-shutters' in the late 12th-century Crusade Cycle poem *Elioxe*. They were probably knee-defences though they might have come from the earlier Byzantine *gonuchlaria*, infantry leg armour. *Poleyn* knee-protections certainly appeared in the mid-13th century, but did not become widespread until the 14th century. They were normally fixed to *cuisses* covering thighs and knees. These were in turn worn over or under the mail *chausses* and became normal items of kit in the later 13th century. Fan-shaped wings on the sides of the *poleyns* to protect the outside and back of the knees may date from around 1325 but did not become widespread for several years.

Rigid greaves and *sabatons* for the lower legs and knees may also have been worn at an early date beneath mail *chausses* but rarely appeared on the surface before 1300. A French reference to a demi-greave in 1302 appears to have been fixed to the rest of the leg armour, probably to the *chausses*. Italian and perhaps Cypriot illustrations more commonly show hardened leather greaves. *Sabatons* or armoured shoes, however, remained very rare before 1320.

Helmets went through the most visible changes during this period. At first a round-topped helmet with or without a nasal was most widespread,

Amasra is one of the few safe harbours along the exposed Black Sea coast of Turkey. The walls and gate of its strong citadel are decorated with Genoese heraldic carving. (Author's photograph)

these being 'laced behind' according to some *chansons de geste* and sometimes having a decorated cercle or rim according to the *Crusade Cycle*. The *Crusade Cycle* also provides interesting details about the construction of late 12th–early 13th-century helmets. Some had their *candelabre* (probably the upper rim of a flat-topped great helm) covered in fine gold with gems set in the nasal, or were protected from the sun by large *flanboiant* or *flabboie* pieces of cloth. A little later John d'Arcy was described wearing a peacock feather in his helmet while on the Fifth Crusade. In its fully developed form the great helm was reserved for the knightly élite in both Europe and Outremer, yet its early history remains obscure. Another late 12th-century Crusade Cycle poem known as the *Le Chevalier au Cigne* goes into even more detail. Here the strongest part of such an *elme* was the summit or *maistre*, beneath which were *candelabres*, perhaps the riveted upper rim, then the *fenestral* protecting the face. These helmets still had a nasal which might now have formed the central bar of the *fenestral*, plus a *mentonal* which was probably a chin-strap. Another helmet in *Le Chevalier au Cigne* also included an *uellière*, this rare term possibly referring to eye slits in the face-covering part of the helmet. An allegorical text written by Radulfus Niger in 1187, the year of Saladin's great victory at Hattin, stated that the *viseria* on these great helms covered the eyes, such a *heaume á visière* almost certainly evolving in response to the increased threat from archery. The fully developed great helm which protected the rear and sides of a knight's head was known by 1220, conical versions being seen by the end of that century. But late 13th-century references to a *heaume á vissère* probably meant one having a pivoted movable visor such as those of the early 14th century.

The *bascinet* and *cervellière* were lighter forms of helmet and in the early to mid-13th century seemed virtually interchangeable. Thereafter

RIGHT **Carvings over the church porch of Decani Monastery, AD 1327-35; Kosovo region, Yugoslavia, in the coastal or Alba-nian style. The military equipment also reflects southern Italian influence. (Author's photographs)**

the *cervellière* referred to a close-fitting hemispherical helmet worn over or beneath a mail coif. Like a *bascinet* it could also be worn beneath a great helm. During the later 13th century the two styles diverged, the *bascinet* becoming a light helmet which included protection for the sides and rear of the neck. The mid 14th-century Italian *barbuta*, however, tended to be deeper and eventually protected much of the face. The brimmed war-hat or *chapel de fer* may have persisted in parts of the Mediterranean world since the fall of Rome, or may have been reintroduced in the 13th century by Mongols who had adopted it from the Chinese. Though it was normally associated with non-élite troops, the war-hat was also used by knights, particularly in the hotter climate of Outremer. From 1320 it got noticeably taller in Italy, the Balkans, Byzantium and probably Outremer, the earlier segmented form being phased out in favour of a one-piece type.

Though known earlier, the wider adoption of separate coifs after 1275 led to the disappearance of a side-fastening, chin-covering *ventail*. Instead, separate mail coifs were often laced up the back. Eventually the coif lost its top and became an *aventail* fastened to the rims of *cervelières* or *bascinets*. Various forms of separate neck protection also developed in the later 13th and 14th centuries. A reference to a *baccinet à gorgière de fer* in 1266 and *gorgières de plate* in 1294 could have meant early forms of mail or scale-lined *aventail* or additional items worn beneath, while the *gorgerettes* included in a large sale of armour in 1295 seemed to be collars with fixing straps that went beneath an *aventail*. From then on gorgets became increasingly common, usually being associated with *bascinets*. During the early 14th century the *pizaine* also appeared in the written records, this almost certainly being a larger, perhaps semi-rigid or more substantial form of *aventail*.

Shields were almost invariably of wood, covered in leather and sometimes with a metal or leather rim; hardened leather shields being associated with Muslims. They were held by *enarmes* internal straps and their weight was supported by a *guige* around the neck. By the mid 14th century, however, they were rarely used by heavily armoured knightly cavalry, at least in warfare. The knightly shield was at its largest in the third quarter of the 12th century and from then on generally got smaller, though the large *talevaz* table-like shield was used by lighter cavalry in

Guest-hall, dam and perhaps sugar-processing mill beneath Montfort castle in northern Palestine. (D. Pringle)
BELOW Exterior of the hall and remains of a dam across the Wadi al-Qarn. RIGHT Interior of the great hall at first-floor level.

hotter climates. Large *tabolaccium anglum* shields with angled corners appeared in Italian art and that of Outremer while fragments of an almost rectangular shield have also been found in 14th-century Tarnovo in Bulgaria. Generally speaking, however, the shields of the 13th-century European knightly élite became thicker and shorter.

Developments in swords were less visible but more significant; changes in blades reflecting developments in armour while changes in hilt design were largely a matter of local fashion. Apparently superficial decoration such as gilding, silvering or painting protected sword-hilts from rust while religious and more rarely secular inscriptions on blades protected the weapon from evil influences or proclaimed the name and allegiance of its owner. From the 11th to 15th centuries most European sword-blades were forged from a single bar of mild steel rather than being piled, folded and pattern-welded as in earlier years. A slender but thicker and longer blade appeared in the mid 12th century in response to a more widespread use of armour. Nevertheless they were much the same weight as earlier swords; generally between 1⅓ kilograms. During the 13th century the carrying of two swords appeared in the Crusader States and Spain, the second sword probably being an early version of the heavier sword-of-war. This had a larger grip which permitted a two-handed stroke, though it was not a true two-handed sword. A selection of surviving swords captured during a mid-14th century Mamluk raid on Crusader Cyprus includes normal weapons and heavier swords-of-war as used in all parts of Outremer.

Daggers were not regarded as a necessary item of cavalry equipment in the early 12th century but came into use less than 100 years later, though they did not became standard knightly equipment until the 14th

century. The earliest type was the *mesericorde* or weapon of 'mercy', presumably because it put a wounded foe out of his misery! A larger dagger or short stabbing sword known as a *stocchi* was first seen in mid-13th century southern Italy, probably due to Byzantine or Islamic influence via Outremer. The broad-bladed *baselard* with its distinctive H-shaped hilt may have been related to the French *bazelaire* or *badelaire*, first mentioned around 1300, though the weapon had already been illustrated in Outremer and Italy. Comparable large daggers had, in fact, been used since the 9th century on both sides of the Mediterranean, particularly in Muslim countries.

Unlike other weapons, the knightly lance did not change much. Its haft was usually of ash or apple-wood, though the Crusade Cycle poem *Elioxe* refers to lances of spruce or fir. By the 14th century heavy lances sometimes incorporated a large wooden disc or graper around the haft. This was not to protect the hand but was held against the armpit to stop a lance being thrust backwards by the shock of impact. In Western Europe and Outremer maces were an élite weapon from their first appearance in the late 11th century. This was still the case by the late 12th century, but from then on the heavy flanged mace became an increasingly popular armour-breaking weapon. One of the most colourful descriptions of a gigantic European knight with a mace comes from the mid 13th-century *Danishmandnamah* Turkish epic:

> *His stature surpassed a hundred arshin*
> *And he carried in his hand a mace*
> *Weighing one hundred and sixty batman and*
> *In its haft were embedded three rocks each weighting forty batman.*

European and Middle Eastern horse-harness and saddlery were very different, the western knight's war-saddle developing into a massive structure which not only made its user ride virtually standing in his stirrups but held him rigidly around his groin and buttocks. Such

equipment provided plenty of scope for rich decoration. Items which the early 14th-century Hospitallers of Cyprus were denied, were precisely those in which more fashionable knights of Outremer delighted, including saddles covered with fine silk cloth. The broad *peytral* or *poitral* breast-strap which stopped a war-saddle from slipping backwards with the jar of impact could be wrapped to go round the entire saddle in the late 12th and 13th centuries, making it even more secure. Secular knights again liked to decorate this and other straps of their horse-harness with gold, silk embroidery and metallic plaques called *lorain*, in addition to painting their coats-of-arms on their saddles.

Horse armour had been widely used in the Middle East since late Roman times, despite the fact that it could cause problems of over-heating. Whether it was reintroduced to Western Europe via the Crusades remains a matter of debate. The Crusader propagandist Radulfus Niger writing in 1187 named the parts of a horse armour as the *testeriam*, head-protection later more generally known as a *chamfron*, the *coleriam* for neck and shoulders, and the *cruperiam* for the rear. Although

Interior of the north wall of the Crusader castle of Androusa, Greece. (Photograph A. Bon)

Unnamed early/mid-14th-century effigy in Salerno Cathedral with several pieces of highly decorated hardened leather armour. (Author's photograph)

a fully armoured horse, or *equus armigerus et coopertus*, remained rare throughout the 13th century horse armour consisted of chamfrons or *testières* for the head, *crupières* for the rear and *flanchières* for the front and sides of the horse. A detailed French document of 1302, listed horse-covers or *caparisons* that were *gamboisés* or *pourpointé*, padded or quilted, as well as *couvertures de fer* which were almost certainly of mail, and others of *jazeran* being mail-lined and cloth-covered. In addition there were *testières* or *chamfrons* all or partly of mail or hardened leather, some being gilded. Perhaps the padded or quilted horse-covers normally served as lining for mail horse armour. The earliest known European reference to *couvertures de plates* incorporating sheets of metal dates from 1338, though it is unclear what and how much was plated.

'The Byzantines attack Shayzar', *History of Outremer*, northern Italy, c. AD 1291-95. This picture represents Byzantines using items of equipment as yet rare in western Europe but possibly used in Outremer, such as separate mail gauntlets, rowel spurs and bamboo lances. (Bib. Nat., Ms. Fr. 2631, f.205r, Paris)

DISPLAY AND HERALDRY

The knightly class took pride in the quality, appearance and good condition of its military gear. Expensive equipment and lavish fittings and decoration all contributed to a knight's reputation, while poor quality harness and dirty or rusted armour or weaponry were considered a matter of disgrace. The same precepts also held true for their clothing. Young 13th-century knights wore jewelled clothes 'as custom required' while others used fine clothes when travelling 'as proud warriors may wear with honour'. As with their harness and weaponry, the quality of their finery provided a visual demonstration of their status.

Fashions in armour could also demonstrate political allegiance. For example, the highly decorated leather armour of 14th-century Angevin possessions in Italy, the Balkans, Cyprus and of the Angevins' Italian allies probably indicated support for the pro-Papacy Guelph faction against the pro-Imperial Ghibellines. The most elaborate example appears on the effigy of Lorenzo Acciaioli who died in 1353, the Acciaioli family having served the Angevins in Naples, Sicily, Latin Greece and the Holy Land.

Heraldry in Outremer followed the same rules as in Western Europe, though there were regional variations. The use of distinctive *connaissances* had probably been stimulated by an increasing use of face-covering helmets during the second half of the 12th century, a knight's *connaissances* also being applied to his pennon, shield, surcoat and as smaller decorative details on his horse-harness and weaponry. The *Roman de Troie*, written around 1160, celebrated such display:

Weapons new and well rounded,
   Helmets, hauberks, shields and saddles
All of a colour the same,
   Which are thus pleasing to their lord,
And by which they know each other.

The 13th-century poem *Galeran* continued this theme when knights prepared for a tournament:

'Siege of Shayzar', *Universal History of William of Tyre*, Acre, c. AD 1284. The soldiers on the right illustrate the light equipment including round shields adopted by knights of Outremer when fighting on foot. (Bib. Nat., Ms. Fr. 9084, f.182v, Paris)

> *Each strives to arm himself with a new clean surcoat.*
> *One has a tower shining brightly on his shield,*
> *One a lion, one a boar, this man a leopard and the other one a fish.*
> *One has a beast or bird or flower on the top of his helmet.*
> *This man bears a sable banner, another white, another blue, another green.*
> *You can see another blazoned with a red coat covered with leaves.*

By the 13th century the knights of Outremer were advised to have their coats-of-arms painted on a horse's *chamfron*, presumably so they could be identified from the front while in a close-packed *conrois* formation. During the mid-14th century the European heraldic system spread beyond Outremer to the indigenous leaders of the Balkans. Here Charles Thopia, ruler of the Albanian principality of Durres, incorporated the French *fleurs-de-lys* into his coat-of-arms, partly because his mother was Helen of Anjou and partly as a mark of allegiance to the Angevin rulers of southern Italy. The *fleurs-de-lys* also spread further and still forms the basis of the Bosnian national flag.

Meanwhile heraldic motifs were used as crests on larger forms of great-helm. For example, some of the leaders of Emperor Frederick II's army in Cyprus had metallic-looking mitres on their helmets, perhaps as a means of identifying senior commanders. The inclusion of a crowned helmet surmounted by a lion in the royal arms of Cilician Armenia similarly indicates a strong western influence via the Crusader states.

THE PLATES

A: ARMS AND ARMOUR, C. AD 1190

1 The Latin states had not yet developed distinctive aspects to their arms, armour and costume. With the possible exception of a cloth around this man's helmet he could have come from anywhere in Western Europe. **2a** Segmented and framed spangenhelm with a broad nasal. **2b** Helmet from beneath, showing leather lining. **2c** Section through helmet and lining, showing partial padding. **3a** Mail coif with ventail unlaced to show soft leather lining and lacing system. **3b** Side of coif with ventail in place, indicating padding between coif and skull. **4a** Quilted *gambeson*. **4b** Strip of printed Egyptian cotton fabric sewn around lower edge of *gambeson*. **5** Mitten of mail hauberk, showing slit leather palm. **6** Example of late 12th/early 13th-century western European fabric such as would be used for ordinary garments. **7a** Quilted mail-lined *chausses* worn over plain woollen hose and cotton breeches. A simple knife or dagger has hypothetically been thrust into the right leg. **7b** Soft leather soles beneath feet of *chausses*. **8a** Gilded prick-spur seen from outside of foot. **8b** Top view of strap and buckle securing the spur. **9** Decorated outer and plain inner surfaces of the metallic chape of sword-scabbard. **10a** Outer face of a leather-covered, gesso-embossed wooden scabbard. **10b** Inner face of scabbard. **11** Detail of pattern on scabbard. **12a** Rawhide sword-belt showing the way its two elements are attached to a scabbard. **12b** Detailed side view of belt and scabbard showing the way in which the two elements are tied to one another. **13a** Gilded iron sword-hilt. **13b** Side view of pommel and grip, showing lacing of leather covered grip. **13c** Section through grip showing iron tang at centre, two pieces of wood around tang and leather covering of grip. **13d** End of gilded iron quillons in the form of a simplified beast's head. **13e** Top view and section through quillons. **13f** Tang of sword-blade with hilt removed, showing tip beaten to secure hilt. **14a** Outside of heraldically painted leather-covered wooden shield with fluted iron boss. **14b** Section across shield. **14c** Inside of shield. **14d** Detail of rivet to secure *enarmes* and *guige* straps. **14e** Vertical profile of shield. **15** Lance-head.

B: *CONROIS* TRAINING C. AD 1200

A *conrois* exercising outside the walls of a Crusader city in Palestine. The unit consists of 20 to 24 men, two ranks deep, with the riders so close that their legs touch. The second rank is less than a horse's length behind the first and has its lances aimed between the riders in front. They are cantering, not galloping or trotting.

C: MALE COSTUME, MID-13TH CENTURY

1a The main figure has the baggy white linen breeches worn beneath all other garments and tightened by a draw-string. **1b** Hems of the breeches could be laced up high, as shown here, or much lower. **2a** Woollen hose, cut on the bias, are worn over the breeches and are tied to the waistband of the breeches. **2b** A later system of securing the hose used a button on the front of the breeches. **2c** Another system added a leather strap to the top of the hose. **2d** Cloth garters were sometimes decorated with brass medallions and strap-ends knotted at the front of the leg. **3** Various styles of soft leather shoes. **4** Various styles of stiff leather boots. **5** Wooden pattens worn over boots or shoes when walking in wet weather. **6** Shirt worn over the breeches and decorated with strips of embroidered material. **7** Front-slit tunic worn over shirt. **8** Alternative side-slit tunic. **9** Fashionable long sleeve of tunic with cuffs folded back to show lining material. **10** Detail of fabric with heraldic rosette pattern. **11** Fuller form of tunic or shirt known as a *bliaut*, sometimes of rich silk and decorated with embroidery. **12** Short tunic with extravagantly long slit sleeves. **13** Simple form of supertunic to be worn over an ordinary tunic. **14** *Garnache* of heavy woollen material, sewn partially up the sides to leave wide armholes and broad flap-like lapels. **15** *Gardecorps* weatherproof hooded garment of heavy woollen fabric. **16a** Plain white linen coif tied beneath chin. **16b** Small simple form of hood. **16c** Later form of hood with short *liripipe* at back. **16d** Buttoned form of hood with long *liripipe*. **16e** Hood with 'dagged' edge; here worn only on top of the head and held in place by a padded *liripipe* around the head. **16f** Dark felt hat with elongated brim at front. **16g** Dark felt hat with upturned brim slit at front and back, worn over hood with a short *liripipe*. **16h** Soft, light-coloured cloth hat worn over a coif. **16i** Broad-brimmed straw hat worn over a coif. **16j** Dark felt beret with decorated lining turned up around the edge; worn over a coif.

D: BATTLE OF NICOSIA, CYPRUS, 1229

During the civil war between an Imperial army from Italy sent by Frederick II and Ibelin forces from the Kingdom of Jerusalem, a close-combat mélée took place on a recently ploughed field, but there was so much dust that the outcome was unclear for some time. During the fighting a Lombard knight in the Imperial army was killed by John of Beirut because he was not wearing a new form of helmet with a face-covering mask or visor.

St Theodore, Cilician Armenian, possibly 14th century. Despite strong Crusader influence on the military élite of Cilicia, this horseman is shown in a purely traditional manner. (Archaeological Museum, Tarsus)

E: ARMS AND ARMOUR, C. AD 1285

1 The figure shown here wears clothes made of rich silk from the neighbouring Muslim states and has weaponry reflecting distinctive styles seen in Outremer during the final years of the Kingdom of Jerusalem. These include a brimmed *chapel-de-fer* helmet, a sword hung from a baldric rather than a sword-belt, an early form of *baselard* dagger and a light oval shield suited to siege warfare on foot. **2** Front and side views of a thickly quilted coif to be worn beneath a mail coif. **3** Type of separate mail coif to be worn beneath a brimmed *chapel-de-fer*, having a padded leather-covered padded ring around skull to support the helmet. **4** Mail coif to be worn beneath a great helm, its almost flat topped shape resulting from a thickly padded arming cap worn beneath. This later form of mail coif also has a broad facial opening which could be tightened across the chin by a draw-string. **5a-c** Front, side and sectional views of a great helm showing the leather lining The helmet is made of five sheets of riveted iron and painted with the owner's heraldic motif. The space between the lining and the top of the helmet might be thickly stuffed straw or horse-hair. **6** Detail of fabric for surcoat, incorporating the knight's coat-of-arms. **7a** Cuirass or pair of plates. **7b** Cuirass when unbuckled and laid flat showing the flap-like cloth skirts, the outer layer of coloured fabric and a leather backing partially removed to show the vertical hardened leather plates. **8** Waist-belt with alternating enamelled heraldic bronze shields and bronze stiffeners riveted to the leather belt. **9a** Leg defences consisting of mail chausses with padded linings worn over the hose, beneath quilted cuisses with domed hardened leather poleyns sewn or riveted permanently on the knees. The mail chausses have leather soles. **9b** Detail of cuisses with integral poleyns, showing lacing down inside of leg and lace through the lower edge. **10** Quilted *aketon* with raised collar buttoned at each side. **11** Interior of oval shield showing plain leather *guige*

and padded squab behind *enarmes* arm straps, the topmost of which was held in the fist. **12a** Scabbard for a light sword and attachment to a baldric. **12b** Side-view of a leather-covered wooden scabbard with flared opening for the sword; baldric removed. **12c** Rear-view of top of scabbard with lacing for baldric attachment. **12d** Detail of lacing system to fasten baldric. **13a** Light sword with 75cm blade, probably for use on foot. **13b** Constituent parts of the sword's hilt, consisting of the tang of the blade, thong to sew leather covering over the wooden grip, the leather covering itself, large-headed short-shafted brass nails around the grip, two halves of the wooden grip with a groove for the tang, the polished bronze quillons with a tapering hole for the tang, enamelled bronze pommel seen from the front and side, and a detail of the pattern on one lobe of the pommel. **14** Flanged iron mace, about 75cms total length, with a wooden grip and leather wrist-strap. **15a** Large sword of war. **15b** Silvered iron pommel with enamelled red cross in centre. **15c** Silvered iron quillons. **16a** Sword-belt and lacing system for the scabbard of a large sword-of-war. (Note: this is not being worn by the figure, since he has a light sword on a baldric.) **16b** Single bronze stiffener from belt with hole for buckle-prong. **16c** Single bronze stiffener from belt without buckle hole. **16d** Upper part of the scabbard with complex lacing system in place. **17a-b** Front and rear of a scabbard for large sword-of-war. **17c** Top of scabbard with reinforcing piece of leather and flaps of thick oiled fabric from the lining. **18** Early form of baselard dagger and sheath.

F: CAPTURE OF THE MINBAR FROM THE MOSQUE AT NABLUS, AD 1242

Attacks on cultural targets were one way in which the declining Crusader states attempted to keep their neighbours at bay. On this occasion a small force of knights led by a band of Templars attacked Nablus, massacring much of the population and seizing the minbar or pulpit from the Great Mosque. It was then taken to Jaffa as a trophy.

G: SUGAR FACTORY-FIEF IN THE KINGDOM OF JERUSALEM, C. AD 1280

Many fiefs in Outremer raised money from industry or commerce rather than agriculture as in Western Europe. Amongst the richest were money-fiefs which included sugar-processing factories. This technology had been copied from the Islamic peoples of the Middle East but, unlike their Muslim neighbours, the Latin élite of Outremer often used slave labour to turn the huge stone presses. Such slaves included captured Muslim women.

H: HORSE HARNESS, EARLY 13TH/MID-14TH C

1 A destrier or war-horse saddled for war or tournament. **2** A destrier with the style of one-piece horse armour used in Outremer and other parts of the Middle East. **3a** Basic wooden frame of a war-saddle. **3b** War-saddle complete with padded leather seat, painted leather covering, doubled girth, breast-strap and stirrups. **3c-e** Front, rear and sectional side views of bronze stirrup. **3f** Alternative method of securing a war-saddle with the breast-strap around the rear of the cantle. **3g** Alternative arrangement of girths, plus padded squabs on the front of the saddle to protect rider while jousting. **4a** Heavy form of curb bit, plus bridle. **4b** Top view of the mouth-piece. **5** Iron horse-shoe. **6** Fully armoured destrier war-horse with two sets of reins; one of leather-covered chain for use in battle, one of ordinary leather straps. 7 Destrier with a later form of war-saddle in which the seat curved up into the *arcons* of the cantle, these in turn wrapping around the rider's buttocks and upper thighs rather than hips. This type of saddle was starting to appear in the mid-14th century but became more widespread later. 8 Early style of deep-seated war-saddle. 9 Later style of war-saddle. 10 Underneath and side views of a horseshoe for a large destrier, showing nails beaten over outside the hoof. 11 *Chamfron* head-protection for a destrier, with the outer decorative layer removed to show a hypothetical reconstruction of the iron frame, sheets of hardened leather, semi-domed iron eye-piece and thick quilted lining. 12a-c Various types of 14th-century stirrups. 13 Elaborate form of iron curb-bit with leather bridle removed. 14 Simple iron snaffle bit with cheek-pieces.

I: TOURNAMENT ON ISTHMUS OF CORINTH, AD 1302

The tournament on the Isthmus of Corinth in the spring of 1302 was an elaborate affair with knights and squires coming from all over Latin Greece. Amongst those who attended were seven champions dressed in green taffeta covered in golden scales, while the ladies of Greece 'rained influence' upon the combatants. When the young Duke of Athens met the older and more experienced Master William Bouchart in single combat, a spiked crest on the chamfron of Bouchart's horse pierced the duke's horse, throwing the duke to the ground.

J: ARMS AND ARMOUR, C. AD 1340

1 The early and mid-14th century was one of the most decorative periods in the history of European armour, particularly when gilded hardened leather protections were used. This figure is based on various sources from the Kingdom of Cyprus, the Angevin realm in southern Italy, Greece and the south-western Balkans. 2 *Cervellière* close-fitting helmet worn beneath a mail coif and a large visored *bascinet*. 3a-b Side and rear views of the mail coif showing tightening strap around the head, lacing up the back and the outline of the collar of a padded tippet and *gambeson* worn beneath. 4 Front of the visored *bascinet* with visor lowered. The cockerel shaped crest would be made from wood, leather and gesso. 5 *Gambeson* consisting of two layers of white linen with thick quilting between. The lower sleeves and skirt are not padded. 6 Mail *haubergeon*, or short-sleeved hauberk. 7 Tippet with thick quilted lining to stop chaffing. 8a Coat-of-plates reconstructed from a mid-14th century example found in the ruins of the Genoese trading outpost of Azov on the Black Sea. Here the armour is shown opened with its red velvet covering removed to show the iron plates riveted to a soft leather backing. 8b The back of the armour opened and laid flat with its velvet covering removed. 8c The front of the armour closed, as when worn, with its velvet outer surface in place. The coat-of-plates was held in place by substantial leather straps plus an iron pin and leather loop on the left shoulder. The removable pin through two iron loops on the chest form a fastening point for guard-chains leading to sword and dagger. 9a Hardened leather, partially gilded *rerebrace* for the upper right arm. 9b *Vambrace* for the lower right arm made of iron splints between layers of leather, plus laces on the outside of the elbow to attach a disc-shaped *besagew*. 9c-d

Upper and lower views of a gauntlet for the left hand, consisting of iron plates on a leather glove with an additional buff-leather protection around the wrist. 10 Embroidered design, largely of gold thread, across chest and back of the surcoat. 11a Leg armour consisting of mail *chausses*, domed iron *poleyns*, quilted *cuisses* with a fringe of mail around the lower edge, an additional sheet of hardened leather to protect the thighs, and highly decorated hardened leather greaves. 11b Outside of the right leg with full leg harness and spur. 11c Outside of right leg with *cuisse* and additional piece of hardened thigh protection removed. 12 Gilded iron spur of revolving rowel type. 13a *Ballock* dagger in its sheath. 13b Side view of *ballock* dagger out of sheath. 13c Side view of velvet-covered wooden sheath; gilded chape and bronze mounts with enamelled coat-of-arms and knotted cord to belt. 14a Sword and scabbard with sectional views of blade and gilded iron quillons. 14b Velvet-covered wooden scabbard with enamelled coat-of-arms on the gilded mounts. 14c New Italian grip method of holding sword with the forefinger over one quillon. 15a Front of double-curved shield with a lance rest. 15b Horizontal section through the shield showing normal curvature around arm and body. 15c Vertical section through the shield showing forward thrusting curvature. 15d Interior of shield.

K: THE NAVAL LANDING AT SMYRNA IN AD 1344

The attack on Smyrna (now Izmir) was one of the most ambitious and successful naval assaults in the later Middle Ages. It was also carried out in the face of fierce Turkish resistance on the beaches. The Crusader knights and other troops emerged from their ships fully armed, the vessels almost certainly being specialized horse-transporting galleys with entry ports in the stern.

COLLECTIONS

Basically there is nothing to collect from the Crusader states. Occasionally a fragment of pottery supposedly dating from the Crusader period turns up in a Middle or Near Eastern bazaar but otherwise surviving artefacts are so rare that even the wealthiest collectors are frustrated. The following is a list of the most important museums and libraries containing material connected with 13th–14th-century Outremer:

ARMS AND ARMOUR

Art Museum Philadelphia, USA: *Cypriot sword from Alexandria Arsenal*

Askeri Museum, Istanbul, Turkey: *Cypriot swords from Alexandia Arsenal*

Metropolitan Museum of Art, New York, USA: *Crusader sword pommel, weapons fragments from Montfort Castle*

Royal Armouries, Tower of London, England: *Cypriot sword from Alexandria Arsenal*

CARVINGS

Arab Ahmet Mosque, Nicosia, Cyprus: *effigial slabs*

Archaeological Museum, Adana, Turkey: *effigial slab*

Archaeological Museum, Limassol, Cyprus: *effigial slabs*

Archaeological Museum, Tarsus, Turkey: *Carving of warrior saint from Armenian church*

Armenian Church, Nicosia, Cyprus: *effigial slabs*

Aya Sofia Mosque, Nicosia, Cyprus: *effigial slabs*

Cathedral, Famagusta, Cyprus: *effigial slab*

Church of St John Vladimir, Elbasan, Albania: *coat-of-arms of Charles Thopia*

Emerghieh Mosque, Nicosia, Cyprus: *effigial slabs*

Serail Mosque, Nicosia, Cyprus: *effigial slabs*

Victoria & Albert Museum, London, England: *marble tympanum from Larnaca*

Yilanlikale, Turkey: *carving over castle gate*

COINS AND SEALS

Bibliothèque Nationale, Cabinet des Medailles, Paris, France

ICONS

Byzantine Museum, Athens, Greece

Museum of the Archbishop Makarios Foundation, Nicosia, Cyprus St Catherine's Monastery, Sinai, Egypt

MANUSCRIPTS

Biblioteca Antoniana, Padua, Italy: 'Book of Psalms' (Ms. C.12)

Biblioteca Medicea-Laurenziana, Florence, Italy: 'History of Outremer' (Ms. Plut. LXI.10)

Bibliothèque de l'Arsenal, Paris, France: 'Arsenal Bible' (Ms. Ars. 5211)

Bibliothèque Municipale, Boulogne, France: 'History of Outremer' (Ms. 142)

Bibliothèque Municipale, Dijon, France: 'Universal History of William of Tyre' (Ms. 562)

Bibliothèque Nationale, Paris, France: 'Universal History of William of Tyre' (Ms. Fr. 9084; & Ms. Fr. 20125)

Bibliothèque Royale, Brussels, Belgium: 'Faits des Romains' (Ms. 10212)

British Library, London, England: 'Histoire Universelle' (Ms. Add. 15268)

Matenadaran Library, Yerevan, Armenia: 'Armenian Gospels' (Ms. 97 &, Ms. 6288, Ms. 7651)

State Public Library, St Petersburg, Russia: 'History of Outremer' (Ms. Fr. Fol. v.IV.5)

Vatican Library, Rome: 'Universal History of William of Tyre' (Ms. Pal. Lat. 1963)

WALL PAINTINGS

Archaeological Museum, Tartus, Syria

Chapel of Castle of Crac des Chevalier (Hisn al Akrad), Syria

Chapel of Marqab Castle, Syria

Church of Panagia Phorbiotissa, Asinou, Cyprus

Church of St Nicholas tis Steyis, Nicosia, Cyprus

Church, Qar'a, Syria

Monastery (abandoned) of Mar Musa, Nebeq, Syria

Monastery of Kalopaneyiotis, Cyprus

Monastery of Mar Charbel, Ma'ad, Lebanon

Monastery of Mar Phocas, Ami'un, Lebanon

Monastery of Mar Sa'ba, Eddeh, Lebanon

Monastery of Mar Tadros, Bahdeidat, Lebanon

BIBLIOGRAPHY

Abulafia, D.S.H., edit., *Commerce and Conquest in the Mediterranean, 1100-1500* (London 1993)

Airaldi, G., & B.Z. Kedar, edits., *I Comuni Italiani nel Regno Crociato di Gerusaleme* (Genoa 1986)

Arbel, B., B. Hamilton & D. Jacoby, edits., *Latins and Greeks in the Eastern Mediterranean after 1204* (London 1989)

Atiya, A.S., *The Crusade in the Later Middle Ages* (London 1938)

Balard, M., *La Mer Noire et la Romanie Génoise (XIIIe–XVe siècles)* (London 1989)

Ben-Ami, A., *Social Change in a Hostile Environment: The Crusaders' Kingdom of Jerusalem* (Princeton 1969)

Bennett, M., 'La Règle du Temple as a military manual, or how to deliver a cavalry charge', in C. Harper-Bill, et al., edits., *Studies in Medieval History Presented to R. Allen Brown* (Woodbridge 1989), pp.7-19

Benvenisti, M., *The Crusaders in the Holy Land* (Jerusalem 1970)

Boase, T.S.R., edit., *The Cilician Kingdom of Armenia* (New York & Edinburgh 1978)

Bon, A., *La Morée Franque* (Paris 1969)

Brundage, J.A., *The Crusades, Holy War and Canon Law* (London 1991)

Chamberlayne, T.J., *Lacrimae Nicossienses: Recueil d'inscriptions funéraires* (Paris 1894)

Charanis, P., 'Piracy in the Aegean during the reign of Michael VIII Palaeologus', *Annuaire de l'Institut de Philologie et d'histoire orientales et slaves* X (1950), pp.127-36

Chehab, M.H., 'Tyr à l'epoque des Croisades', special volume of Bulletin du Musée de Beyrouth, XXXI (1979)

Ducellier, A., *La Façade Maritime de l'Albanie au Moyen Age: Durazzo et Valone du XIe au XVe siècle* (Thessaloniki 1981)

Edbury, P.W., *The Kingdom of Cyprus and the Crusades 1191-1374* (Cambridge 1991)

Eydoux, H-P., L'architecture militaire des Francs en Orient', in J.P. Babelon, edit., *Le Château en France* (Paris 1986), pp.61-77

Fedden, R. & J. Thomson, *Crusader Castles* (London 1977)

Geanakoplos, D.J., 'Greco-Latin Relations on the Eve of the Byzantine Restoration: The Battle of Pelagonia – 1259', *Dumbarton Oaks Papers*, VII (1953), pp.99-141

Holt, P.M., edit., *The Eastern Mediterranean Lands in the Period of the Crusades* (Warminster 1977)

Housley, N., *The Later Crusades, 1274-1580; From Lyons to Alcazar* (Oxford 1992)

Hyland, A., *The Medieval Warhorse from Byzantium to the Crusades* (Stroud 1994)

Jacoby, D., *Recherches sur la Mediterrannée Orientale du XIIe au XVe Siècle* (London 1979)

Jacoby, D., *Société et Démographie à Byzance et en Romanie Latine* (London 1975)

Jacoby, D., *Studies on the Crusader States and on Venetian Expansion* (London 1989)

Kedar, B.Z., *The Franks in the Levant, 11th to 14th Centuries* (London 1993)

Kedar, B.Z. et al., edits., *Outremer: Studies in the Crusading Kingdom of Jerusalem Presented to Joshua Prawer* (Jerusalem 1982)

Lowe, A., *The Catalan Vengeance* (London & Boston 1972)

Luttrell, A., *Latin Greece, the Hospitallers and the Crusades 1291-1400* (London 1982)

Marshall, C.J., 'The French Regiment in the Latin East, 1254-91', *Journal of Medieval History*, XV (1989), pp.301-7

Marshall, C.J., 'The Use of the Charge in Battles in the East, 1192-1291', *Historical Research*, LXIII (1990), pp.221-6

Marshall, C.J., *Warfare in the Latin East, 1192-1291* (Cambridge 1992)

Mayer, H.E., *Kings and Lords in the Latin Kingdom of Jerusalem* (London 1994)

Miller, W., *The Latins in the Levant: A History of Frankish Greece (1204-1566)* (London 1908)

Nicholson, H., 'Knights and Lovers: The Military Orders in the Romantic Literature of the Thirteenth Century', in M. Barber, edit., *The Military Orders: Fighting for the Faith and Caring for the Sick* (Aldershot 1994), pp.340-5

Pascu, S., edit., *Colloquio Romeno-Italiano 'I Genovesi nel Mar Nero durante i secoli XIII e XIV' (Bucharest 27-28 Marzo 1975)* (Bucharest 1977)

Prawer, J., *Crusader Institutions* (Oxford 1980)

Prawer, J., 'Crusader Cities', in H.A. Miskimin et al., edits., *The Medieval City* (New Haven 1977), pp.179-99

Pryor, J.H., *Geography, Technology and War: studies in the maritime history of the Mediterranean 649-1571* (Cambridge 1988)

Pryor, J.H., 'In Subsidium Terrae Sanctae: Exports of food-stuffs and war material from the Kingdom of Sicily to the Kingdom of Jerusalem, 1265-1284', *Asian and African Studies*, XXII (1988), pp.127-46

Richard, J., *Le Comté de Tripoli sous la Dynastie Toulousaine* (Paris 1945)

Richard, J., *Croisades et Etats Latins d'Orient* (London 1992)

Richard, J., *Croisés, missionaires et voyageurs* (London 1983)

Richard, J., *The Latin Kingdom of Jerusalem* (Oxford 1979)

Riley-Smith, J., *The Feudal Nobility and the Kingdom of Jerusalem 1174-1277* (London 1973)

Thiriet, F., *La Romanie Vénitienne au Moyen Age* (Paris 1955)

GLOSSARY

AILETTES: shoulder-pieces solely for heraldic display

AKETON: quilted soft-armour originally of cotton

ARCHONS: ex-Byzantine military élite in Latin Greece

ASGERGUM: *see hauberk*

AVENTAIL: mail attached to the rim of a cervelière or bascinet helmet

BACCINET: *see bascinet*

BAÇILLETUM: *see bascinet*

BADELAIRE: *see baselard*

BAILI: government's military representative

BARBATA: early meaning probably of coif or aventail

BARBERIA: mail coif

BARBUTA: deep form of bascinet protecting much of the face

BASCINET: light helmet also covering sides and rear of head

BASCINETTO: *see bascinet*

BASELARD: dagger with distinctive H-shaped hilt

BAYLIA: *see baili*

BAZELAIRE: *see baselard*

BESAGEWS: discs protecting elbow

BOHORDEIS: individual jousting

BRAS DE FER: early form of upper arm protection

BRIGANDINE: flexible form of cuirass consisting of very small plates

CALICAS FERREIS: leg armour

CALIGAS: boots or greaves

CANDELABRE: probably the upper rim of a flat-topped great helm

CAPARISON: horsecloth covering all or most of the animal

CAPELLO DE FERRO: *see war-hat*

CAPIRONE DE FERRO: *see coif*

CAPPELUM DE ACCIARIO: *see war-hat*

CERCLE: lower rim of helmet

CERVELIÉRE: light hemispherical helmet

CERVELLIÈRE: *see cervelière*

CHAMFRON: armour for head of horse

CHANSON DE GESTE: warlike poem or song

CHAPEL DE FER: *see war-hat*

CHATELAIN: commander of a castle

CHAUSSES: mail stockings

CHEVAUCHÉE: raid

CHICANE: early form of polo in France

CLAVAIN: neck and shoulder protection

CLIPEUM: shield

COAT-OF-PLATES: segmented body armour attached to a leather or fabric base

COIF: flexible head-protection

COLERIAM: armour for neck and shoulders

CONNAISSANCES: heraldic emblems

CONNÉTABLE: second ranking royal military officer of state

CONROIS: cavalry formation

CORAZINIIS: *see cuirass*

CORAZZA: *see cuirass*

CORELLUS: *see cuirass*

COUTEAU: dagger

COUTER: armour for elbow

COUVERTURES: fabric covering for horse

COUVERTURES DE FER: mail horse-armour

COUVERTURES DE PLATES: plated horse-armour

CRUPERIAM: *see crupière*

CRUPIÈRE: armour for rear of horse

CUIR-BOUILLI: hardened leather

CUIRASS: plated body-armour

CUIRIE: body armour of buff leather

CUISSES: armour for thighs and knees

CULTELLUM DE FERRO: dagger

CURACIJS: *see cuirass*

DESTRIER: war-horse

DUBBING: knighting ceremony

ECHELLES: squadrons

ECU: shield

ENARMES: holding straps of shield

EPAULIÈRE: see espalière

ESPALIÈRE: shoulder armour

FALDIS SPONTONEM: armour for abdomen

FENESTRAL: part of helmet protecting face

FERRO GAMBERIAS: leg armour

FIEF: piece of land or other economic entity supporting a knight

FLABBOIE: *see flanboiant*

FLANBOIANT: piece of cloth on helmet

FLANCHIÈRE: armour for front and side of horse.

GAMBERUOLIS: leg armour.

GAMBESON: form of soft-armour

GENELLIÈRE: probably knee protection

GONFANONIER: standard-bearer

GORGÈRE: *see gorgèrettes*

GORGÈRETTES: neck protection

GORGIERA: *see gorgèrettes*

GORGIÈRE : *see gorgèrettes*

GORGIÈRE DE PLATE: scale-lined aventail or neck protection

GRAPER: wooden disc round haft of lance

GREAT HELM: heavy helmet covering entire head

GREAVES: armour for lower leg

GUIGE: supporting neck-strap of shield

HAUBERGEON: short-sleeved mail armour

HAUBERK: mail shirt of tunic

heaume à visière: helmet with fixed or movable face protection

INDULGENCE: certificate given by the Church, forgiving sins in return for specified penance

JUPEAU D'ARMER: form of padded armour from the Turco-Arabic jubbah quilted armour

LAMERIAS: early form of cuirass

LAMERIAS VEL CORACZAS: *see coat-of-plates*

LAMIÈRES: early form of cuirass

LANCEAM: lance

LATTEN: metal alloy similar to brass

LORAIN: decorative metallic plaques on horse-harness

MAHONESI: assocation of ship-owners, merchants and/or knights governing Genoese colonial outposts

MAISTRE: summit of helmet

MANICIS CIROTECAS DE FERRO: arm defences

MARÉCHAL: ruler's third-ranking military official

MENTONAL: probably a chin-strap

MESERICORDE: dagger

MITTENS: *see mufflers*

MUFFLERS: mail protection for hands

NASAL: nose-protecting extension of helmet

OSBERGUM: *see hauberk*

PAIR OF CUIRASSES: *see cuirass*

PAIR OF PLATES: *see coat-of-plates*

PALFREY: riding horse not used in battle

PANCERIA: form of hauberk

PANCERIAM, pansière, panzeria,

PANZERIAM: *see panceria*

PAVISES: large infantry shield

PERPUNTO GROSSO ET CONSCIALIBUS FERREIS: quilted armour with iron lining probably of scales

PEYTRAL: breast-strap of horse-harness

PIZAINE: larger, perhaps semi-rigid form of aventail

PLATES: *see coat-of-plates*

plates de alemayne: see coat-of-plates

POITRAL: *see peytral*

POLEYN: knee-protection

POULAINS: name given to knight of mixed European and Middle Eastern parentage

POURSUIVANT: new knight or 'learner'

QUINTAINE: revolving target used in training with lance

QUIRET: probably buff leather body-armour

REREBRACE: armour for upper arm

RESTOR: system whereby the King of Jerusalem replaced value of horses or military equipment lost when knights served outside the Kingdom

SABATONS: armoured shoes

SCHINERIAS: *see greaves*

SCUTO: *see scutum*

SCUTUM: shield

SÉNÉCHAL: senior military government official

SOLERETS: *see sabatons*

SOVOSBERGANI: probably a form of early cuirass

SPATAM: sword

ABOVE **The fortress of Moncastro in the Ukraine (also known as Cetatea Alba, Ak Kirman and now called Bilhorod Dnistrovs'kvi) was first built by the Genoese to guard the estuary of the Dnister river. It is seen here in a 19th-century Russian print. (Kiev Historical Museum photograph)**

SPAULDER: *see espalière*

SQUIRE: knight's servant, or member of nobility beneath knight (meaning varies)

STIVALETTI: *see chausses*

STOCCHI: larger dagger or short stabbing sword

SUMPTER: pack-horse

SURCOAT: garment worn over armour

TABOLACCIUM: large form of shield

TABOLACCIUM ANGLUM: shield with angled corners

TABOLATUM: large form of shield

TALEVAZ: largest form of shield

TARGE: kite-shaped shield

TARGIAM: *see targe*

TARIDA: specialized horse-transporting galley of Arab origin

TAVOLACCIO: see tabolaccium

TESTERIAM: head armour for horse

TROUBADOUR: poet and singer

UELLIÈRE: possibly eye slits in the face-covering part of a helmet

VAMBRACE: armour for lower arm

VENTAIL: flap of mail on coif to protect chin

VOLET: decorative 'veil' tied around helmet

WAR-HAT: brimmed helmet

INDEX

(References to illustrations are shown in **bold**)